WILDERNESS

ROCKWELL
ALASKA MCMXVIII

R.K.

WILDERNESS

A JOURNAL OF QUIET ADVENTURE
IN ALASKA

BY ROCKWELL KENT

FOREWORD BY DOUG CAPRA

INCLUDING EXTENSIVE HITHERTO UNPUBLISHED
PASSAGES FROM THE ORIGINAL JOURNAL

WESLEYAN UNIVERSITY PRESS

Published by University Press of New England
Hanover and London

UNIVERSITY PRESS OF NEW ENGLAND publishes books under its own imprint and is the publisher for Brandeis University Press, Dartmouth College, Middlebury College Press, University of New Hampshire, University of Rhode Island, Tufts University, University of Vermont, Wesleyan University Press, and Salzburg Seminar.

Wesleyan University Press
Published by University Press of New England, Hanover, NH 03755

© 1996 by Wesleyan University Press
Foreword © 1996 by Doug Capra

Reprinted by arrangement with the Rockwell Kent Legacies from the 1970 edition published by the Wilderness Press. First published in 1920.

Cover illustration: Rockwell Kent, *Resurrection Bay, Alaska*, 1965 from 1919 sketch. Oil on canvas, 71 x 111.8 cm. Gift of ATZ Travel, ERA Helicopters, Dr. and Mrs. Lloyd Hines, Bruce Kendall, and Alyeska Pipeline Service Company. Anchorage Museum of History and Art 73.3.1. Photo by Chris Arend.

Detail of Alaska Steamship Co. map on p. xxxvi originally published in 1917 by Poole Bros., Chicago. Courtesy of Doug Capra.

LIBRARY OF CONGRESS CATALOGING-IN-PUBLICATION DATA

Kent, Rockwell, 1882–1971.
　Wilderness: a journal of quiet adventure in Alaska / by Rockwell Kent; Foreword by Doug Capra.
　　p.　cm.
　Originally published: Rev. ed. Los Angeles: Wilderness Press, 1970. With new foreword.
　ISBN 0-8195-5293-3 (alk. paper)
　1. Renard Island (Alaska)—Description and travel. 2. Renard Island (Alaska) in art. 3. Kent, Rockwell, 1882–1971. 4. Artists—Alaska—Biography. I. Title.
F912.R39K3　1996
917.98'4—dc20
95-45450

To old L. M. Olson and

young Rockwell Kent

of Fox Island

this journal is respectfully dedicated

FOREWORD

Doug Capra

For seven short months—between late August 1918 and mid-March 1919—Rockwell Kent and his nine-year-old son, also named Rockwell, lived on a small island in Resurrection Bay not far from Seward, Alaska. Their host and companion, a seventy-one-year-old Swede and Alaskan pioneer named Lars Matt Olson, described himself as "noting bott a brokendown Freunters Man." Lonely, and too old to prospect and trap as in his youthful days, Olson welcomed the Kents to his island home, where he ran a small fox and goat farm.

Kent chronicled his adventures on Fox Island in this, his first book, which was published in 1920 to stellar reviews. *The New Statesman* said it was "easily the most remarkable book to come out of America since *Leaves of Grass.*" *The Chicago Post* wrote: "the artist who can put into the simplest drawings of a man and a little boy eating together at a rough table in a rough cabin all the dear solidity of family and home life—that artist can make me bow my head before his sincerity."

Wilderness is perhaps Kent's most charming and lasting literary accomplishment. Robert Benchley in the *New York World* first summed up its almost mythical qualities: "Those who come back to the unlovely haunts of men after such a sojourn . . . bring with them something which makes them the envy of all urbanites. This something Rockwell Kent has brought back from Alaska and put into *Wilderness.*" The gift Kent brought back from the Alaskan wild was nothing less nor more than himself, his own artistic voice and vision. "It seems," Kent writes, "that we have . . . turned out of the beaten, crowded way and come to stand face to face with that infinite and unfathomable thing which is the wilderness; and here we found OURSELVES—for the wilderness is nothing else."

Since its publication, *Wilderness* has stirred the imaginations of countless artists, writers, and adventurers and influenced more than one of them to venture to Alaska. It is a book about art and life, about alienation and integration, about the inner life, the spiritual life, the simple life; and it is about growing old gracefully, without losing one's childhood ideals. In *Wilderness,* Kent confronts the emptiness and loneliness of the abyss and fills it with the richness and wealth of his soul.

Almost nothing of the personal life Kent left in New York, nor his experiences in the town of Seward, is included in *Wilderness*. This missing information adds much to an understanding of his life and gives us an interesting glimpse between the lines of what is written here. For Kent does leave us clues. In the preface to the first edition, he writes: "Deliberately I have begun this happy story far out in Resurrection Bay;—and again dropped its peaceful thread on the forlorn threshold of the town." Olson, and others in Seward who read the book, understood this as a reference to Kent's battle with the town. Until recently, however, biographers and readers alike have either overlooked this cryptic remark or wondered at its obscurity.

Born on June 21, 1882, in Tarrytown Heights, New York, Rockwell Kent was a child of wealthy late-Victorian society. His father died when Kent was five years old, leaving him little more than his silver flute. Kent carried that flute with him throughout his life—to Newfoundland, Alaska, Tierra del Fuego, and Greenland. After his father's death, the family floundered between periods of affluence and genteel poverty, dependent on the charity of wealthy relatives.

Kent rebelled early, as an account of his private schooling shows, but his mother's sister, a talented artist herself, nurtured his artistic gifts. Kent wanted to paint, but his practical family advised him to pursue a career as an architect. He studied architecture at Columbia University, but perfected his painting under mentors Abbott Thayer, William Merritt Chase, and Robert Henri. He eventually dropped out of Columbia to pursue his painting full time.

In 1905, Henri introduced Kent to the rugged cliffs of Monhegan Island off the coast of Maine, twenty miles from Boothbay Harbor, marking the artist's early experience with the solitude of island life. He lived and painted there, built himself a small house—read Emerson, Thoreau, Dostoevski, Turgenev, Tolstoy, Ruskin, Schopenhauer, Spencer, and Haeckel—and worked as a laborer and lobsterman.

In 1908, Kent married Kathleen Whiting, Abbott Thayer's niece, and began a twelve-year struggle to support his growing family. By 1914, with career and family responsibilities in mind, Kent had journeyed twice to Newfoundland, where he first developed his taste for stark northern climates. He made the first trip alone, in 1910, to Burin, a small town located on a deep fjord with an island-dotted harbor, in search of land for a communal art school he hoped to start with a friend. In 1914, this time with Kathleen and the children, he journeyed to Brigus, a former sealing port located on a small inlet at

viii

the head of Conception Bay. This trip coincided with the outbreak of World War I. Accused of being a German spy, Kent responded by flaunting his love of all things German and his disdain for the town's provincial British attitude. Already in the town's bad graces for his bizarre sense of humor and insensitive practical jokes, he and his whole family were forced to leave the country—Kathleen pregnant and the three other children sick with whooping cough. In the following years Kent struggled to paint and earn a living, depending upon his skills as an architect, designer, and builder.

At thirty-six, Kent considered himself a financial failure. He had shown his paintings successfully and had received promising reviews, but he wondered whether his art would ever be able to support himself and his family. A socialist and pacifist in a money-hungry world at war, he suffered occasional fits of depression and had contemplated suicide. He had even considered moving permanently to Germany. Thus the Alaskan adventure was no artist's junket, but perhaps Kent's last-ditch effort to salvage his career. As he confided to his wife Kathleen: "Never did I enter upon any course with such a sense of necessity, of duty, as drives me into this Alaska trip." He was determined to demonstrate his artistic worth to a hostile world, not just to make it a better place, but to create for himself a secure haven within it.

And yet, he came to Alaska also because he craved solitude and isolation and because he loved the North. "I crave snow-topped mountains, dreary wastes, and the cruel Northern sea with its hard horizons at the edge of the world where infinite space begins. Here skies are clearer and deeper and, for the greater wonders they reveal, a thousand times more eloquent of the eternal mystery than those of softer lands."

The Kents, father and son, arrived in Seward aboard the steamer *Admiral Farragut* shortly after six in the morning on Saturday, August 24, 1918. Kent immediately registered at the Hotel Sexton and began inquiring about a quiet place to locate. Money was tight, and he couldn't afford to stay in a hotel for long. At the Seward Grill, he scanned the menu for the cheapest yet healthiest meal. For two days, the waiter asked whether he wanted soup, coffee, tea, pie, pudding, or any dessert with his meal. Avoiding his son's eyes, he would say no, only to learn later that those items came with the price of the meal!

He hiked inland several miles, but the terrain looked too tame. "I knew at once that we must choose the seacoast to settle upon," he wrote. Through a local photographer, Kent learned about Fox Island, and of the local tinsmith named Graef, who was planning a Sunday berry-picking party along the

Seward at about the time Kent was on Fox Island. Courtesy of the Resurrection Bay Historical Society, Seward, Alaska.

coast of Resurrection Bay. Kent got himself invited, and, while the others picked berries, borrowed a dory and ventured out into the Bay with his son. He describes his trip and his meeting Olson in the opening chapter of *Wilderness*.

An excellent carpenter, Kent's design and construction skills paid off throughout his life. On Fox Island, he converted one of Olson's goat houses into comfortable living quarters, cleaning it out, chinking the walls with moss and clothing, and furnishing it for the simple life. Kent also added a west-facing two-by-two-foot window to the small cabin. Olson's partner, Thomas W. Hawkins, "grub staked" Kent by supplying him with some materials and food. A versatile businessman and Seward booster, Hawkins was gambling that Kent's art would help promote Seward. In thanks, Kent painted an oil on plywood portrait of Hawkins's daughter, Virginia, from a photograph. The Seward Chamber of Commerce, also excited to have a New York artist in town, encouraged Kent. In the Kent papers at the Archives of American Art in Washington, D.C., is the draft of a letter written in Kent's hand. It is an introduction and recommendation, supposedly from the Seward

Rockwell Kent on Fox Island. Courtesy of the Rockwell
Kent Legacies.

Chamber of Commerce, but drafted by Kent himself. He probably planned
to use the letter to obtain free travel accommodations in Alaska. Apparently,
he had hoped the chamber would sign it, but their relationship soured and
Kent never finished the letter.

Kent—who was to embark upon a series of affairs on his way to a third and
successful marriage—had begun a new relationship with a German girl
named Gretchen before coming to Alaska. Kathleen had known, and now
Kent was afraid she would leave him. Both, it seems, wanted a reconciliation.
Still, she refused to join him in Alaska, understandable considering her miserable Newfoundland experience. At one point, Kent even considered taking Gretchen, but rejected the idea in favor of his son Rockwell. Kathleen
didn't want the boy to go, but Kent fought desperately to take him despite his
wife's objections. Kathleen finally relented, perhaps realizing that the boy

served as a lifeline for their marriage. Though Kent continued his correspondence with Gretchen while on Fox Island, he also wrote to Kathleen that the affair was over. Gretchen had helped comfort him through his suicidal depressions, but her love was never a threat, he assured Kathleen. In her letters, Kathleen complained of her loneliness and suggested there were local men interested in her.

While on Fox Island, Kent had recurring nightmares about another man seducing his wife and feared desperately that she would leave him. Despite his own unfaithfulness, he warned her: "I think for jealousy I could kill a man. No—for jealousy I could kill myself." There is a subtext to *Wilderness* that occasionally reveals the Kent who, enthralled with the paradise around him, was living through an inner hell. "I have terrible moments, hours, days

Rockwell Kent's cabin on Fox Island. Photo by Rockwell Kent. Courtesy of the Rockwell Kent Legacies.

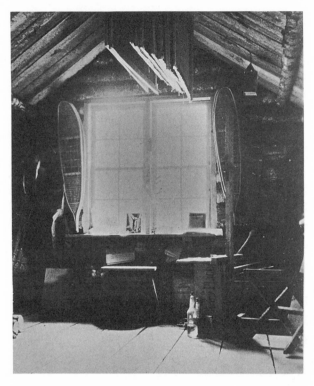

The interior of Rockwell Kent's cabin on Fox Island.
Note the paintings hanging from the ceiling and the work
in progress on his makeshift desk. Photo by Rockwell
Kent. Courtesy of the Rockwell Kent Legacies.

of homesick despondency . . . for my family," he wrote. "There are times
when if I could I'd have fled from here in any raging storm."

Kent kept in touch with the art world through his friend Carl Zigrosser,
editor of the Ferrer Associaton magazine, *The Modern School*. They shared
their philosophy of life and art, and their disillusionment with a barbarous
world. He also wrote to his wife, to Gretchen, and to his children. He
cooked, played his flute, painted, cut wood, hiked over the island, read
William Blake and Friedrich Nietzsche, occasionally visited friends in town,
played with and read to his son, and enjoyed listening to Olson's stories. Olson's genuine fondness for his guests and his gentle roughness touched the
artist. Kent described him as a man who, "If his eye troubled him seriously,
would stick in his finger and pull the eye out—and then doubtless fill the

socket with tobacco juice." Despite what was happening in the world at home, Kent vigorously pursued his art. Delighted with the work he was producing, he gradually regained confidence. He wrote to a patron: "I begin to see a purpose to it all, a direction, and to believe profoundly in my own destiny."

During this time, his name occasionally appeared in the Seward newspaper. In September, he is listed with sixty-five others who donated to a relief fund for the starving Armenians. His one dollar contribution no doubt taxed his limited resources. In December, he wrote a letter to the Chamber of Commerce that appeared in the *Seward Gateway* complaining about the poor mail service. He had left a Seward forwarding address in Yakutat, his first stop in Alaska, yet four months later he still hadn't received important materials, probably canvas, shipped from New York in August. In late March, Kent wrote a short article for the newspaper titled *Pets and Paradise*, in which he describes life on Fox Island and praises his friend Olson.

In chapter 7 of *Wilderness*, under a December 14 entry, Kent mentions that Olson finally brought over a letter the older man had written to Kathleen. "The letter is full of nice humor," Kent writes. What he doesn't tell us is that, desperate to convince Kathleen to come to Alaska, he had urged Olson to write the letter.

Mr. Kint and me heav bing talking over difrens subjakt and in regard to you making a trip to alaska. you heav a god exchus. you Husband and your son ar hear now. probly efter som time you vil not heav so god chans. and i tank a trip like this wold du you a great deal of god. a trip like this wold be out roffing at. and a change from City life . . . expanses ar vary small. ve heav no rant to pay, no Coal Bill or Watter bill. alectricity—50 cts per gallon. Locomocion—50 cts for 4 hours. the only trubly ve heav ar ve heav to Cot Down a tre ons avile saw at an split at and pack at in to the Hous and put at enta the Stove.

In chapter 11, Kent mentions that Kathleen was amused at Olson's brusque ending: "you Can ancer this letter if you fel lik at and if you Dunt all the seame to me." That's the way it is here in Alaska, Olson had told him. "If anyone don't like the way a man does he can go to Hell!" He doesn't tell us that Olson also wrote: "Mr. Kint vonted me to Whrit to you so you most not bleam me for et."

Despite Olson's charm, Kathleen refused to join her husband and son. She wanted them to return to New York. As winter turned to spring, Kent re-

Olson and his goats and young Rockwell standing on the porch of Olson's cabin on Fox Island. Photo taken by Rockwell Kent. Courtesy of the Rockwell Kent Legacies.

alized he had better leave to save his marriage. "I bitterly regret leaving this wonderful free spot," he wrote Zigrosser, "just as the fairer weather approaches and I begin to see the true wonderland that surrounds this bay." Kent worked frantically those last months on Fox Island, half finishing projects that he would complete later. "I've no idea what I'll do on reaching New York," he wrote. Olson, disappointed that father and son had to leave so early, told him that he might as well have spent a couple of months back in the mountains of New York for all he'd seen of Alaska. Kent's depression returned. "I have often thought it over and weighed carefully the choice of . . . quitting life entirely, and I never came to any satisfactory conclusion. I wonder how the damned business will end."

Rockwell Kent and his son left Fox Island on March 17, 1919, and stayed in Seward for almost two weeks. On March 27, the *Seward Gateway* published Kent's farewell letter. "You have a manhood in this land that is rare," he wrote. "Men who are here because by their initiative and force they differed from the rest of men. . . . Every law that limits their freedom in their own affairs is tyranny." Kent goes on to warn Seward to beware of the dry rot and contamination already within the community—the prohibitionists; and those who would forcibly register and draft a free people into military service. Beware, he warned, of busybodies who mind everyone's business but their own. "Militarists in lamb's clothing," he calls them, and then compares them to the German Kaiser, Wilhelm. Despite these potential dangers, Kent ends by praising Alaska as "the only land that I have ever known to which I wanted to return."

The front page of the next day's *Seward Gateway* featured a letter from local public school teacher, Mary Wright, with the headline: "Wanted—An Explanation." Apparently, on one of Kent's trips to town, his son had visited the school as a guest of his host's children. During recess, some other children dragged him before Miss Wright as she read a book. "Tell her what flag you like best," they taunted. "The German," he replied. The teacher tapped him gently on the hand with her book and told him he'd "better not speak that way around here." At the time, she thought it was only a practical joke. But later, another teacher told her that young Kent had also said: "I don't hate any flag but the English." Miss Wright was shocked to learn that this lad was the "son of an eccentric artist from New York living on an island near Seward." Not only had he never attended public school, but he also spoke some German. "Mr. Kent," she ended her letter. "Where did your boy get these ideas?"

A few years before he died, I talked with Kent's son, Rockwell, at his Uxbridge, Massachusetts, home. He recalled this event vividly yet differently. The teacher had passed around a *Book of Knowledge* and the children were asked to select their favorite flag. Young Kent, fascinated with Alaska's eagles, had quickly found a flag featuring that intriguing bird. Far from his mind was the thought that this particular bird represented the German imperial eagle.

Still, only months after World War I had ended, talk like this was considered blasphemous, almost treasonous. Seward had reacted like many small towns to the war, entrenching itself in patriotic fervor and anti-German sentiment. Local militias met two or three times a week for drill; a Four-Minute Club organized to fight pro-German propaganda; rumors spread of German spies around every corner; the local newspaper heralded stories about German atrocities and barbarism; German books in public schools and libraries were burned or stored away; and anyone speaking the language or singing German was considered suspect. Kent had learned in Newfoundland the dangers of flaunting his love of German culture. He had tried to remain low key in Seward, though he still befriended and socialized with many of the town's German-Americans.

The day after Miss Wright's letter appeared, the *Seward Gateway* published Kent's reply on the front page. It is an eloquent letter, defending children's integrity and their right to have an opinion; confessing love for the English flag; condemning an unimaginative public school system; pleading for forgiveness on both sides now that the war was over; and answering the teacher's question: "I don't know where my son gets any of his ideas."

Knowing that he would leave for New York the next morning, Kent took a parting shot at Seward: "On the eve of my departure," he wrote, "it has taken a teacher from Indiana to furnish me with one reason why a man with children to educate should not return to Seward." In its struggle for economic survival, Seward was striving to attract settlers. Kent knew how to hit the town where it hurt.

Kent left Seward aboard the *Admiral Farragut* on March 30, 1919. Two Alaskan shows at the Knoedler Gallery in New York—one within a month after his return, the second timed to coincide with the publication of *Wilderness*—were both artistic and financial successes. Even four of young Rockwell's drawings sold in the first show. Kent's friends convinced him to publish a book based on his journals, letters, and art work. So he retreated to Vermont with his family to write. On September 2, Kent wrote to Olson in Seward: "My book is in the hands of the publishers, but it will not come out until next winter. I've set down Seward about as Seward deserves. And my dear old friend, I've paid you part of the tribute you deserve."

Kent did not include the German flag incident in *Wilderness*, and for good reasons. With anti-German sentiment still strong, and the "Red Scare" in progress, Kent no doubt realized the book would be unpublishable with such a chapter. "In the fervor of post-war patriotism," Kent wrote in his preface to a later Modern Library edition, "my original publisher . . . secretly deleted and subsequently would not put back . . . two lines of a German folksong." It is unusual, however, that Kent did not mention the Seward incident in his 1955 autobiography, or to my knowledge, in any of his letters.

In Vermont, he missed Alaska fiercely and resented his forced early departure. "I can't think of Fox Island without being a bit homesick," he wrote to Olson, and encouraged the old man, who had recently suffered a slight stroke, to come live with him in Vermont. Olson agreed, and after several fundraisers, including a dance sponsored by the Seward chapter of the Pioneers of Alaska, and with some money Kent had wired him—Olson left for

Vermont. Unfortunately, Olson arrived at just the wrong time. Kent, feeling restless and confined, longed for another adventure. He was lashing out at all around him. Olson's presence reminded him of the wonder, beauty, and solitude of Fox Island, and that made things worse. Shortly after Olson's arrival, he and Kent got into a petty argument over how to wean a calf. Both were too stubborn to give an inch.

Olson packed up and headed out West where his youthful adventures had begun. He eventually set up a lone homestead in an isolated spot near Jackson Hole, Wyoming. He died in the fall of 1922—alone—as he had lived most of his life. "His remains were discovered," the local paper reported, "by persons who chanced to pass by." Although no one knows its occupant, there is an unmarked grave near his Wyoming homestead.

The success of his Alaska art work and his first book, as Kent later wrote, "began a period of such financial security as Kathleen and I had hitherto not known. . . . I could now paint. The immediately following years were to be the most consistently productive of my life." Indeed, as soon as Kent had settled in Vermont, an idea he originated on Fox Island bore fruit. He became a business and sold shares in *Rockwell Kent Incorporated*, though he soon bought out his investors. Throughout the 1920s and 1930s, he became one of American's most respected illustrators and graphic artists, creating books about his new travels to Tierra del Fuego and Greenland.

Controversy followed Kent throughout his life, and he often encouraged it. He was an avowed socialist and often accused of being a communist, though he never joined the party. Wherever he saw injustice he was moved to help. He traveled to Brazil to protest against government torture and murder; he supported the leftists in the Spanish Civil War; he became chairman of the National Council of American-Soviet Friendship in the midst of the Cold War. But Kent never forgot Fox Island. He was so charmed by that Christmas of 1918 on a remote Alaska island that he excerpted those chapters from *Wilderness* and published them in 1941 in a little volume called *A Northern Christmas*.

In 1953, Kent was subpoenaed by Senator Joseph McCarthy's Permanent Subcommittee on Investigation to answer for his leftist leanings. McCarthy's committee intended to destroy two of Kent's books housed in overseas government libraries—*Wilderness* and *N by E*—because they were considered subversive. This incident, among others, had much to do with Kent's later decision to donate the bulk of his paintings and other works to Russia, including the manuscript to *Wilderness*. They now reside at the Pushkin Fine

Arts Museum in Moscow and at the Hermitage in St. Petersburg. In America, the most complete and balanced collection of Kent's work can be found at the Rockwell Kent Gallery in the Plattsburgh Art Museum in Plattsburgh, New York.

On March 13, 1971, after a final fight of eleven unconscious days and nights, Rockwell Kent died. He is buried at Asgaard, his farm in upstate New York, beneath a large block of Vermont granite that bears a favorite line from Walter Scott—also the title of Kent's book about his America: "This is My Own."

For more Information

The Kent Collector is a quarterly magazine published by the Rockwell Kent Gallery, SUNY-Plattsburgh Art Museum, Plattsburgh, N.Y. 12901. For more details about Rockwell Kent's visits to Alaska, see the following issues with articles by Doug Capra: Fall, 1985; Winter, 1985; Summer, 1986; Winter, 1989; Fall, 1994.

Books of interest include:

Johnson, Fridolf. *Rockwell Kent: An Anthology of his Works*. New York: Alfred A. Knopf, 1982.

Kent, Rockwell. *It's Me O Lord: The Autobiography of Rockwell Kent*. New York: Dodd, Mead & Co., 1955.

Traxel, David. *An American Saga: The Life and Times of Rockwell Kent*. New York: Harper & Row, 1980.

The Resurrection Bay Historical Society Museum in Seward has a Kent display that includes a scale model of the Fox Island cabin.

Doug Capra

Seward, Alaska
April 1995

PREFACE

Most of this book was written on Fox Island in Alaska, a journal added to from day to day. It was not meant for publication but merely that we who were living there that year might have always an unfailing memory of a wonderfully happy time. There's a ring of truth to all freshly written records of experience that, whatever their short-comings, makes them at least inviolable. Besides the journal, a few letters to friends have been drawn upon. All are given unchanged but for the flux of a new paragraph or chapter here and there to form a kind of narrative, the only possible literary accompaniment to the drawings of that period herein published. The whole is a picture of quiet adventure in the wilderness, above all an adventure of the spirit.

What one would look for in a story of the wild Northwest is lacking in these pages. To have been further from a settled town might have brought not more but less excitement. The wonder of the wilderness was its tranquillity. It seemed that there both men and the wild beasts pursued their own paths freely and, as if conscious of the freedom of their world, molested one another not at all. It was the bitter philosophy of the old trapper who was our companion that of all animals Man was the most terrible; for if the beasts fought and killed for some good cause Man slew for none.

Deliberately I have begun this happy story far out in Resurrection Bay;—and again dropped its peaceful thread on the forlorn threshold of the town. We found Fox Island on Sunday, August twenty-fifth, 1918, and left there finally on the seventeenth of the following March.

R. K.

Arlington, Vermont,
   December, 1919.

A SECOND PREFACE

Eleven Years Later

And the thought that was born to me in the quietness of that adventure—
that in the wilderness, in uneventful solitude, men for companionship
must find themselves—has come to be for me the truth. Maybe the only
truth I know.

Go, young men to grow wise and wise men to stay young, not West
nor East nor North nor South, but anywhere that men are not. For we
all need, profoundly, to maintain ourselves in our essential, God-descended
manhood against the forces of the day we live in—to be at last less prod-
ucts of a culture than the makers of it. There, in that wilderness so an-
ciently unchanged it might have seen a hundred cultures flower and die,
there realize —you must—that what is you, what feels and fears and hun-
gers and exalts, is ancient as the wilderness itself, rich as the wilderness
and kin to it. And of those ancient values of the soul, Art through all its
fashions of utterance, despite them all, despite the turmoil of this age,
despite New York and Harlem, steel and jazz, proclaims above the riot of
Godlessness that there, in Man, eternally, is all the very much man ever
knew of God.

Privileged by conviction to confirm, as I have, my thoughts of years
ago, I am again privileged by the broad-mindedness of the proprietors of
the Modern Library to restore to the following journal two lines of a German folk-song that my original publisher (later the publisher of the prof-
itable effusions of Emil Ludwig), in the fervor of post-war patriotism,
secretly deleted, and subsequently would not put back. They are on page
68, and mean: "Good moon, you go so quietly through the evening clouds."

I have been asked why Olson (read the book) stayed away so long.
No reason. There was never much reason for anything. He wanted to.

R. K.

Au Sable Forks, N.Y. 1930

THIRD PREFACE

The "quiet adventure" of fifty years ago of which *Wilderness* is the story is vested in my fond thoughts with something of the glamour and, perhaps, the wisdom of *Robinson Crusoe* and *The Swiss Family Robinson*. "Father," said to me a balding, six-foot-four tall scientist, "the year we spent together on Fox Island was the happiest of all my life."

"Of mine, too, Sonny," I might have added but for loyalty to my whole long past and the "adventures," both quiet and unquiet, that had somehow come to fill it.

Of the three human beings who shared as one that speck of earthly Paradise which is the setting of this journal, only the father and his son remain; while of their habitations nothing is left but rotting logs.

Alaska, now a state, its oil-rich lands and waters on the auction block, who knows what traces of Fox Island's once primaeval wilderness may in the course of time be left. Fearing the worst, to that dear, peaceful wilderness I say a loving, last farewell. "Earth to earth, ashes to ashes, dust to dust. . . . ."

ROCKWELL KENT

"Asgaard"
Au Sable Forks, N. Y. 1970

INTRODUCTION TO ALASKA DRAWINGS
(M. Knoedler & Co. 1919)

Shortly following our return from Alaska in 1919 it was arranged that my drawings (those that were subsequently to be published in WILDERNESS) be shown at the Knoedler Gallery in New York; and that for the catalog the eminent art critic, Dr. Christian Brinton, was to write the Introduction.

Dr. Brinton was so pleased with what at his request I wrote him that he found no words by himself to be necessary, merely suggesting that it be printed as an IMAGINARY LETTER to himself. This, he assured me, would be "a brilliant journalistic trick." And so it was that as a writer I first broke into print.

Fox Island, Resurrection Bay, Alaska,
Winter,1919.

Dear Dr. Brinton:

It is difficult to know what to write down for you, as it has always been hard for me to understand myself, to know *why* I work and love and live. Yet it is fortunate that such matters find a way of caring for themselves. I came to Alaska because I love the North. I crave snow-topped mountains, dreary wastes, and the cruel Northern sea with its hard horizons at the edge of the world where infinite space begins. Here skies are clearer and deeper and, for the greater wonders they reveal, a thousand times more eloquent of the eternal mystery than those of softer lands. I love this Northern nature, and what I love I must possess.

The Northern wilderness is terrible. There is discomfort, even misery, in being cold. The gloom of the long and lonely winter nights is appalling and yet do you know I love this misery and court it. Always I have fought and worked and played with a fierce energy, and always as a man of flesh and blood and surging spirit. I have burned the candle at both ends and can only wonder that there has been left even a slender taper glow for art. And so this sojourn in the wilderness is in no sense an artist's junket in search of picturesque material for brush or pencil, but the fight to freedom of a man who detests the petty quarrels and bitterness of the crowded world—the pilgrimage of a philosopher in quest of Happiness!

But the wilderness is what man brings to it, no more. If little Rockwell and I can live in these vast silences beside the heartless ocean, perched high up on the peak of the earth with the wind all about us, if we can stand here and not flee from the terror of emptiness, it is because the wealth of our own souls warms the mountains and sea, and peoples the great desolate spaces. For the time we look into ourselves and are not afraid. We find here life, true life—life rich, resplendent, and full of love. We have learned not to fear destiny but to live for the heaven that can be made upon earth.

Often I think that however much I draw or paint, or however well, I am not an artist as art is generally understood. The abstract is meaningless to me save as a fragment of the whole, which is life itself. I can only see line as a human gesture, a gesture that has no value apart from what it signifies. It is the ultimate which concerns me, and all physical, all material things are but an expression of it. In planning a picture I am as one who merely plays his appointed part. If I draw superman he is but the embodiment of my inner and outer vision, a creature huge and glorious, striding over towns and cities, rivers and mountain peaks, with arms outstretched, raised high into the luminous abyss. Is this art? I do not know—or care.

We have searched hard, my Kathleen and I, for the Great Happiness. Yet I can readily see that the struggle would have been for nothing without the constant hope of peace before all is over. Always we seem, at least to ourselves, to gather a little more wisdom along the pathway to some wonderful free land. It is this that we are living for, and art is but the outward record of our progress. You'll know, Christian Brinton, when our goal has been reached. And the "show" for which I trust you may some day prepare the catalogue shall be called "Paintings of Paradise."

So here you have a sort of profession of faith. We are part and parcel of the big plan of things. We are simply instruments recording in different measure our particular portion of the infinite. And what we absorb of it makes for character, and what we give forth, for expression.

Alaska is a fairyland in the magic beauty of its mountains and waters. The virgin freshness of this wilderness and its utter isolation are a constant source of inspiration. Remote and free from contact with man our life is simplicity itself. We work, work hard with back and hands felling great trees. We row across thirteen miles of treacherous water to the nearest town; and the dangers of that trip, and the days and nights, weeks and months alone with my son during which time I have learned to see *his* wonder-world and know his heart—such things are to me the glory of Alaska. In living and recording these experiences I have sensed a fresh unfolding of the mystery of life. I have found wisdom, and this new wisdom must in some degree have won its way into my work.

Faithfully yours,

ROCKWELL KENT

CONTENTS

ILLUSTRATIONS

THE MAD HERMIT

Lane

Talkeetna R.

Talkeetna

Sunshine

Impoar Pass

Yentna

Deshka R.

Caswell

Jonesville

Eska

Sutton

Granite

Castle

Chickaloon

MATA COAL

Rainy Pass

Skwentna R.

Susitna R.

Houston

ALASKA R.R.

Matanuska R.

Kings Mt.

Mt. Estella 8,700

Beluga

Susitna

Alexander

Knik

Matanuska

CHUGACH

Lake George

Birchwood

ANCHORAGE

Bissell Lake

Beluga

Ladd

Tyoonok

FIRE ID.

Turnagain Bay

Campbell

Rainbow

Granite Mine

Golden

Fork

Old Tyonok

Trading Bay

Kern

PORTAGE

Kustatan

U.S. AGRICULTUBAL EXPERIMENT STA.

Kenai

Skittok

Hope

Grandview

NAKED ID.

Pt. Newell

Prince

Redoubt Bay

KALGIN ID.

Skilah Lake

MTS.

Johnson

Kussiloff

Roosevelt

Tanalian Lake

C. Kasilof

Tustumena Lake

Kenai L.

Lakeview

Chenc

KNIGHT

Iliamna Peak

Tazimina akes

Neuelchuk

Primrose

Woodrow

ALASKA

SEWARD

U.S. COALING STATION

LATO

ILIAMNA

Anchor Pt.

Aurora

Blyings

C. Resurrection Sound

ELRINGTON ID.

Cape C

Iliamna Bay

Dutton

Homer

Bluff Pt.

Kachelmak Bay

Nuka Bay

CHISWELL IDS.

SEAL ROCKS

Kamishak Bay

Mt. Chinabora

AUGUSTIN ID.

Pt. Beda

SELDOVIA

Port Graham

Pt. Gore

PYE IDS.

CAPE ELIZABETH

CHUGACH IDS.

SHAW ID.

BARREN IDS.

C. Douglas

USHUGAT ID.

GUL

TTER IDS.

KLUKPALIK ID.

Pt. Banks

CHUYAK ID.

Shuyak Str.

C. Nukhshak

Black C.

C. Current

BAN ID.

C. Tonki

AFOGNAK ID.

C. Paramanof

MARMOT ID.

Ugyak Steep

Malinof St.

C. Pillar

liak

Marmot Bay

SPBERRY ID.

AFOGNAK

BANIK ID.

SPRUCE ID.

KODIAK

Uyak Bay

Chiniak Bay

WILDERNESS

I. DISCOVERY

We must have been rowing for an hour across that seeming mile-wide stretch of water.

The air is so clear in the North that one new to it is lost in the crowding of great heights and spaces. Distant peaks had risen over the lower mountains of the shore astern. Steep spruce-clad slopes confronted us. All around was the wilderness, a no-man's-land of mountains or of cragged islands, and southward the wide, the limitless, Pacific Ocean.

A calm, blue summer's day,—and on we rowed upon our search. Somewhere there must stand awaiting us, as we had pictured it, a little forgotten cabin, one that some prospector or fisherman had built; the cabin, the grove, the sheltered beach, the spring or stream of fresh, cold water,— we could have drawn it even to the view that it must overlook, the sea, and mountains, and the glorious West. We came to this new land, a boy and a man, entirely on a dreamer's search; having had vision of a Northern Paradise, we came to find it.

With less faith it might have seemed to us a hopeless thing exploring the unknown for what you've only dreamed was there. Doubt never crossed our minds. To sail uncharted waters and follow virgin shores— what a life for men! As the new coast unfolds itself the imagination leaps into full vision of the human drama that there is immanent. The grandeur of the ocean cliff is terrible with threat of shipwreck. To that high ledge the wave may lift you; there, where that storm-dwarfed spruce has found a hold for half a century, you perhaps could cling. A hundred times a day you think of death or of escaping it by might and courage. Then at the first softening of the coast toward a cove or inlet you imagine all the mild

3

beauties of a safe harbor, the quiet water and the beach to land upon, the house-site, a homestead of your own, cleared land, and pastures that look seaward.

Now having crossed the bay thick wooded coast confronted us, and we worked eastward toward a wide-mouthed inlet of that shore. But all at once there appeared as if from nowhere a little, motor-driven dory coming toward us. We hailed and drew together to converse. It was an old man alone. We told him frankly what we were and what we sought.

"Come with me," he cried heartily, "come and I show you the place to live." And he pointed oceanward where, straight in the path of the sun stood the huge, dark, mountain mass of an island. Then, seizing upon our line, he towed us with him to the south.

The gentle breeze came up. With prow high in the air we spanked the wavelets, and the glistening spray flew over us. On we went straight at the dazzling sun and we laughed to think that we were being carried we knew not where. And all the while the strange old man spoke never a word nor turned his head, driving us on as if he feared we might demand to be unloosed. At last his island towered above us. It was truly sheer-sided and immense, and for all we could discover harborless; till in a moment rounding the great headland of its northern end the crescent arms of the harbor were about us,—and we were there!

What a scene! Twin lofty mountain masses flanked the entrance and from the back of these the land dipped downwards like a hammock swung between them, its lowest point behind the center of the crescent. A clean and smooth, dark-pebbled beach went all around the bay, the tide line marked with driftwood, gleaming, bleached bones of trees, fantastic roots and worn and shredded trunks. Above the beach a band of brilliant green and then the deep, black spaces of the forest. So huge was the scale of all of this that for some time we looked in vain for any habitation, at last incredulously seeing what we had taken to be boulders assume the form of cabins.

The dories grounded and we leapt ashore, and followed up the beach onto the level ground seeing and wondering, with beating hearts, and crying all the time to ourselves: "It isn't possible, it isn't real!"

There was a green grass lawn beneath our feet extending on one side under an orchard of neatly pruned alders to the mountain's base, and on the other into the forest or along the shore. In the midst of the clearing stood the old man's cabin. He led us into it. One little room, neat and

"Zarathustra himself led the ugliest man by the hand, in order to show him his night-world and the great round moon and the silvery water-falls nigh unto his cave"

5

comfortable; two windows south and west with the warm sun streaming through them; a stove, a table by the window with dishes piled neatly on it; some shelves of food and one of books and papers; a bunk with gaily striped blankets; boots, guns, tools, tobacco-boxes; a ladder to the store-room in the loft. And the old man himself: a Swede, short, round and sturdy, head bald as though with a priestly tonsure, high cheek-bones and broad face, full lips, a sensitive small chin,—and his little eyes sparkled with good humor.

"Look, this is all mine," he was saying; "you can live here with me—with me and Nanny,"—for by this time not only had the milk goat Nanny entered but a whole family of foolish-faced Angoras, father, mother, and child, nosing among us or overturning what they could in search of food. He took us to the fox corral a few yards from the house. There were the blues in its far corner eying us askance. We saw the old goat cabin built of logs and were told of a newer one, an unused one down the shore and deeper in the woods.

"But come," he said with pride, "I show you my location notice. I have done it all in the proper way and I will get my title from Washington soon. I have staked fifty acres. It is all described in the notice I have posted; and I would like to see anybody get that away from me."

By now we had reached the great spruce tree to whose trunk he had affixed a sort of roofed tablet or shrine to house the precious document. But, ah look! the tablet was bare! only that from a small nail in it hung a torn shred of paper.

"Billy, Nanny!" roared the old man in irritation and mock rage; and he shook his first at the foolish-looking culprits who regarded us this time, wisely, from a distance. "And now come to the lake!"

We went down an avenue through the tall spruce trees. The sun flecked our path and fired here and there a flame-colored mushroom that blazed in the forest gloom. Right and left we saw deep vistas, and straight ahead a broad and sunlit space, a valley between hills; there lay the lake. It was a real lake, broad and clean, of many acres in extent, and the whole mountain side lay mirrored in it with the purple zenith sky at our feet. Not a breath disturbed the surface, not a ripple broke along the pebbly beach; it was dead silent here but for maybe the far off sound of surf, and without motion but that high aloft two eagles soared with steady wing searching the mountain tops. Ah, supreme moment! These are the times in life— when nothing happens—but in quietness the soul expands.

6

Unknown Waters

Time pressed and we turned back. "Show us that other cabin, we must go."

The old man took us by a short cut to the cabin he had spoken of. It stood in a darkly shadowed clearing, a log cabin of ample size with a small doorway that you stooped to enter. Inside was dark but for a little opening to the west. There were the stalls for goats, coops for some Belgian hares he had once kept, a tin whirligig for squirrels hanging in the gable peak, and under foot a shaky floor covered with filth.

But I knew what that cabin might become. I saw it once and said, "This is the place we'll live." And then returning to our boat we shook hands on this great, quick finding of the thing we'd sought and, since we could not stay then as he begged us to, promised a speedy return with all our household goods. "Olson's my name," he said, "I need you here. We'll make a go of it."

The south wind had risen and the white caps flew. We crossed the bay pulling lustily for very joy. Reaching the other shore we saw, too late, crossing the bay in search of us the small white sail of the party that had brought us part way from the town. So we turned and followed them until at last we met to their relief and the great satisfaction of our tired arms.

1 Olson's Cabin
2 Goat Cabin
3 Fox Corral
4 Kents' Cabin
5 Old feed-house
6 Boats
7 Spring
8 Pond
9 Otter trail
10 Drift-wood

II. ARRIVAL

Our journal of Fox Island begins properly with the day of our final coming there, Wednesday, August the twenty-eighth, 1918.

At nine o'clock in the morning of that day we slid our dory into the water from the beach at Seward, clamped our little patched-up three and one half horse-power Evinrude motor in the stern, and commenced our loading.

Since the main part of such a story, as in all these following pages we shall have to tell, must consist in the detailing of the innumerable little commonplaces of our daily lives, we shall begin at once with a list, as far as we have record of it, of all we carried with us. It follows:

1 Yukon stove	10 lbs. rice
4 lengths stovepipe	5 lbs. barley
1 broom	10 lbs. cornmeal
1 bread pan	10 lbs. rolled oats
1 wash basin	10 lbs. hominy
1 bean pot	10 lbs. farina
1 mixing bowl	10 lbs. sugar
Turpentine	50 lbs. flour
Linseed oil	2 packages bran
Nails, etc.	6 cans cocoa
10 gals. gasoline	1 lb. tea

1 case milk
8 lbs. chocolate
1 gal. sirup
1 gal. cooking oil
1 piece bacon
2 cans dried eggs
2 cans baked beans
6 lemons
2 packages pancake flour
10 lbs. whole wheat flour
6 Ivory Soap
3 laundry soap
6 agate cups
4 agate plates
4 agate bowls
2 agate dishes
4 pots
2 pillows
2 comforters
1 roll building paper
1 frying pan
3 bread tins

10 lbs. lima beans
10 lbs. white beans
5 lbs. Mexican beans
10 lbs. spaghetti
12 cans tomatoes
100 lbs. potatoes
10 lbs. dried peas
5 lbs. salt
1 gal. peanut butter
1 gal. marmalade
Pepper
Yeast
5 lbs. prunes
5 lbs. apricots
5 lbs. carrots
10 lbs. onions
4 cans soup
12 candles
2 Dutch Cleanser
Matches
1 tea kettle
Pails, etc.

Also there were a heavy trunk containing books, paints, etc., one duffel bag, one suit case, and a few other things. And when these were stowed away in the dory there was little room for ourselves. However, at ten o'clock we cast off and started for Fox Island with the little motor running beautifully.

It lasted for three miles when at once, with a bang and a whir, the motor raced, and the boat stood motionless on the calm gray water. Through the fog we could just discern the cabin of a fisherman on the nearest point of shore—perhaps a mile distant. We rowed there as best we could, seated somehow atop our household goods; we unloaded our useless motor, our gasoline, and our batteries, cleared a little space in the boat for ourselves to man the oars, and in a miserable drizzling rain, pushed off for a long, long pull to the island. By too literal a following of directions I lengthened the remainder of the course to twelve miles, and that we rowed, I don't know how, in four hours and a half. Fortunately the water was as calm

Home Building

as could be. Rockwell was a revelation to me. With scarcely a rest he pulled at the heavy oars that at first he had hardly understood to manage; and when we reached the island he was hilarious with good spirits.

We unloaded with the help of Olson—whom by the way we must introduce at some length—and stowed our goods in his house and shed. We cooked our supper on his stove and slept that night and the next on his floor; and then, having our own quarters by that time in passable shape, quit his friendly roof for the most hospitable, kindly, and altogether comfortable roof in the world, our own.

Olson is about sixty-five years of age. He's a pioneer of Alaska and knows the country from one end to the other. He has prospected for gold on the Yukon, he was at Nome with the first rush there, he has trapped along a thousand miles of coast; and now, ever unsuccessful and still enterprising, he is the proprietor of two pairs of blue foxes—in corrals—and four goats. He's a kind-hearted, genial old man with a vast store of knowledge and true wisdom.

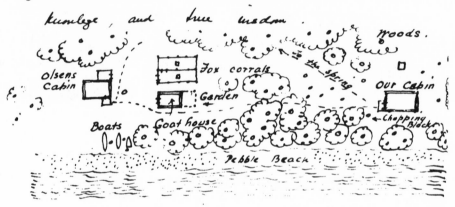

The map shows our Fox Island estate. Our cabin was built as a shelter for Angora goats somewhat over a year ago. It is a roughly built log structure of about fourteen by seventeen feet, inside dimensions, and was quite dark but for the small door and a two by two feet opening on the western side. We went to work upon it the morning following our arrival and in two days, as has been told, made it a fit place to live in but by no means the luxurious home that it was in our mind to make. Our cabin today is the product of weeks' more labor. To describe it is to account for our time almost to the beginning of the detailed days of this diary.

Tread first upon a broad, plank doorstep, the hatch of some ill-fated vessel—the sea's gift to us of a front veranda; stoop your head to four feet

Fire Wood

six inches and, drawing the latchstring, enter. Before you at the south end of the somber, log interior is a mullioned window willing to admit more light than can penetrate the forest beyond. Before it is a fixed work table littered with papers, pencils, paints, and brushes. On each long side of the cabin is a shelf the eaves' height, five feet from the floor. The right-hand one is packed with foods in sacks and tins and boxes, the left-hand shelf holds clothes and toys, paints and a flute, and at the far corner built to the floor in orthodox bookcase fashion, a library.

We may glance at the books. There are:

"Indian Essays." Coomaraswamy
"Griechische Vasen"
"The Water Babies"
"Robinson Crusoe"
"The Prose Edda"
"Anson's Voyages"
"A Literary History of Ireland."
  Douglas Hyde
"The Crock of Gold"
"The Iliad" "The Odyssey"
"Fairy Tales." Andersen
"The Oxford Book of English Verse"

"The Home Medical Library"
"Poems." Blake
"Life of Blake." Gilchrist
"The Tree Dwellers," "The Cave
  Dwellers," "The Sea People," etc.
"Pacific Coast Tide Table"
"Thus Spake Zarathustra"
"The Book of the Ocean"
"Albrecht Dürer" (A Short
  Biography)
"Wilhelm Meister"
"In Northern Mists." Nansen

In the center of the right-hand wall is a small low window and beneath it the dining table. Right at the door where we stand, to our left, is the sheet-iron Yukon stove and behind it another food-laden shelf. A new floor of broad unplaned boards is under our feet, a wooden platform—it is a bed—stands in the left-hand corner by the stove. Clothes hang under the shelves; pots and pans upon the wall, snowshoes and saws; a rack for plates in one place, a cupboard for potatoes and turnips behind the door— the cellar it may be called; the trunk for a seat, boxes for chairs, one stool for style; axes here and boots innumerable there, and we have, I think, all that the eye can take in of this adventurers' home!

Trees stood thick about our cabin when we first came there; and between it and the shore a dense and continuous thicket of large alders and sapling spruces. Day by day we cleared the ground; cutting avenues and vistas; then, though contented at first with these, enlarging them until they merged, and the sun began to shine about the cabin. It grew brighter then and drier,—nonsense! am I mistaking the daylight for the sun? I can remember but one or two fair days in all the three weeks of our first stay on the island.

14

For a true record of this matter Olson's diary shall be copied into these pages. It follows in full with his own phonetic spelling as leaven.

Sunday, Aug. 25th.—Wary fin Day. over tu Hump Bay got 2 salmon an artist cam ar to Day and going to seward efter his outfit and ar going to sta Hear this Winter in the new Cabbin.

Wed. 28th.—Drisly rain and cold. Mr. Kint and is son arivd from seward this afternoon. goats out all night.

Thurs. 29th.—goats cam ome—12:30 P. M. Mr. Kint Working on the Cabbin fixing at up. Drisly rain all night and all day.

Fri. 30th.—Wary fin day and the goats vant for the montane igan. Help putting Windoes i to the Cabbin.

Sat. 31st.—Foggy day. Big steamer going to seward.

SEPTEMBER

Sun. 1st.—Mead a trip around the island. Cloudy Day.

M. 2.—Big rainstorm from the S. E. goats all in the stabel.

T. 3.—Drisly rain all Day.

W. 4.—going to seward.

T. 5.—Came Home 1 P. M.

F. 6.—Drisly rain and Calm Wather.

S. 7.—S. E. rainstorm.

Sun. 8.—Big S. E. rainstorm.

M. 9.—   ” ” ”   ”

T. 10.—   ” ” ”   ”

W. 11.—first Colld night this fall. Clear Calm Day.

T. 12.—Clowdy and Calm. Tug and Barg going West.

F. 13.—Steamer from the Sought 5.30 P. M. Drisly rain and Calm.

S. 14.—raining Wary Hard. the litly angora queen ar in Hit this morning. Fraet steamer from West going to Seward.

Sun. 15.—raining Wary Hard all Day. the goats ar in the cabbin all Day sought Est storm.

M. 16.—S. E. rainstorm.

T. 17.—raining all Day. North Est storm With Caps and Wullys all over.

W. 18.—Wary fear day. Mr. Kint and the Boy vant to seward this morning.

T. 19.—raining heard all day steamer from West going to seward 4 P. M.

F. 20—raining heard all Day.

S. 21.—Wary rof rainstorm from Soght Est. Wullys all over.

Sun. 22.—Steamer from West going to Seward 2 P. M. the tied vary Hie
Comes clear up in the gras and the surf ar Stiring up all the Driftwood
along the shore. raining lik Hell.

M. 23.—raining all Day.

T. 24.—Snow on top of the mountins on the maenland a tre mastid skuner
from West going to Seward. toed by som gassboth raining to Day egan.
Mr. Kint and son got ome to the island this Evening.

September Fourteenth

I stopped writing, for the fire had almost gone out and the cold wind
blew in from two dozen great crevices in the walls. The best of log cabins
need recalking, I am told, once a year, and mine, roughly built as it is,
needs it now in the worst way. Some openings are four or five inches wide
by two feet long. We've gathered a great quantity of moss for calking, but
it has rained so persistently that it cannot dry out to be fit for use.

Well, it rains and rains. Since beginning this journal we've had not
one fair day, and since we've been here on the island, seventeen days,
there has been only one rainless day. There has been but one cloudless
sunrise. I awoke that day just at dawn and looking across out of the tiny
square window that faces the water could see the blue—the deep blue—
mountains and the rosy western sky behind them. At last the sun rose
somewhere and tipped the peaks and the hanging glaciers, growing and
growing till the shadows of other peaks were driven down into the sea
and the many ranges stood full in the morning light. The twilight hours
are so wonderfully long here as the sun creeps down the horizon. Just
think! there'll be months this winter when we'll not see the sun from our
cove—only see it touching the peaks above us or the distant mountains.
It will be a strange life without the dear, warm sun!

I wonder if you can imagine what fun pioneering is. To be in a country
where the fairest spot is yours for the wanting it, to cut and build your
own home out of the land you stand upon, to plan and create clearings,
parks, vistas, and make out of a wilderness an ordered place! Of course
so much was done—nearly all—when I came. But in clearing up the woods
and in improving my own stead I have had a taste of the great experience.
Ah, it's a fine and wholesome life! . . .

Another day. The storm rages out of doors. To-day I stuffed the largest
of the cracks in our wall with woolen socks, sweaters, and all manner of
clothes. It's so warm and cozy here now! Olson has been in to see me for a

The Sleeper

long chat. I believe he can give one the material for a thrilling book of adventure. Take his story, or enough of the thousand wild incidents of it, give it its true setting—publishing a map of that part of the coast where his travels mostly lay—let it be frankly his story retold, above all true and savoring of this land—and I believe no record of pioneering or adventure could surpass it. He's a keen philosopher and by his critical observations gives his discourse a fine dignity. On Olson's return to Idaho in the '80's after his first trip to Alaska a friend of his, a saloon-keeper, came out into the street, seized him, and drew him into his place. "Sit down, Olson," he said, "and tell us about Alaska from beginning to end." And the traveler told his long wonder-story to the crowd.

At last he finished.

"Olson," said his friend, "that would be the greatest book in the world— if it was only lies."

Gee, how the storm rages!

I'm relieved to-night; Rockwell, who seems to have a felon on his finger, is improving under the heroic treatment he submits to. I've had visions of operating on it myself—a deep incision to the bone being the method. It is no fun having such ailments to handle—unless you're of the type Olson seems to be who, if his eye troubled him seriously, would stick in his finger, and pull the eye out,—and then doubtless fill the socket with tobacco.

We have reached Wednesday, September the eighteenth.

That day the sun did shine. We rowed to Seward, Rockwell and I; stopped for the motor that on our last trip we had left by the way, but found the surf too high. At Seward the beach was strewn with damaged and demolished boats from a recent storm. Moreover, in the town the glacial stream was swollen to a torrent; the barriers had, some of them, been swept away; a bridge was gone, the railroad tracks were flooded, the hospital was surrounded and almost floated from its foundations. And we saw the next day, when it again poured rain, the black-robed sisters of charity, booted to the thighs, fleeing through the water to a safer place. It stormed incessantly for four days more. Although I had taken what seemed ample precaution for the safety of my dory, she was caught at the height of the storm by the exceptional tide of that season and carried against a stranded boat high up on the shore, and pinioned there by a heavy pile torn from the wharf. But our boat escaped undamaged.

Seward was dull for Rockwell and me. We've not come this long way

The Windlass

from our home for the life of a small town. America offers nothing to the tourist but the wonders of its natural scenery. All towns are of one mold or inspired, as it were, with one ideal. And I cannot see in considering the buildings of a single period in the East and in the West any indication of diversity of character, of ideals, of special tradition; any susceptibility to the influence of local conditions, nothing in any typical American house or town where I have been that does not say "made in one mill." There's a God forsaken hideousness and commonplaceness about Alaskan architecture that almost amounts to character—but it is not quite bad enough to redeem itself. Somewhere in the wilderness of the Canadian Rockies there's a little town of one street backed up against the towering mountains. Dominating the town is the two- or three-story "Queen Hotel," the last word in flamboyant, gimcrack hideousness. Hotel and Mountain! it is sublime, that bald and crashing contrast.

On September third, I wrote to a friend: "They strike me as needlessly timid about the sea here, continually talking of frightful currents and winds in a way that seems incredible to me and would, I think, to a New England fisherman. However, I must be cautious. Olson says that in the winter for weeks at a time it has been impossible to make the trip to Seward. Well, I'll believe it when I try it and get stuck."

Three weeks later,—Tuesday, September twenty-fourth, we were in Seward. The morning was calm varying between sun and rain, but it seemed a good day to return to Fox Island. Rockwell and I had some difficulty launching our boat down the long beach at low water; but at last we managed it, loaded our goods aboard,—viz., two large boxes of groceries, fifty-nine pounds turnips, a stove, five lengths of stovepipe, a box of wood panels, two hundred feet one inch by two inch strips, suit case, snowshoes, and a few odd parcels.

At ten forty-five we pushed off. At just about that moment the sun retired for the day and a fine and persistent rain began to fall. After about three miles we were overtaken by a fisherman in a motor sloop bound to his camp three miles further down the shore. He took us in tow and, finally arriving at his camp, begged us to stay "for a cup of tea"—he was an Englishman. I yielded to the delay there against my own better judgment. After a hearty meal we left his cove at two fifteen.

Still it drizzled rain and the breeze blew faintly from the northeast. We had a seven-mile row before us. Near Caines Head we encountered squalls from the south and were for some time in doubt as to the wind's true direction. We headed straight for Fox Island only to find the wind easterly, compelling us to head up into it. I fortunately anticipated a heavier blow and determined to get as far to windward and as near the shelter of the lee shore as possible, and without any loss of time. Our propulsion toward the island I left to the tide which was about due to ebb. We made good headway for a little time until the wind bore upon us in heavy squalls.

The aspect of the day had become ominous. Heavy clouds raced through the sky precipitating rain. The mountainous land appeared blue-black, the sea a light but brilliant yellow-green. Over the water the wind blew in furious squalls raising a surge of white caps and a dangerous chop. I was now rowing with all my strength, foreseeing clearly the possibility of disaster for us, scanning with concern the terrible leeward shore with its line of breakers and steep cliffs. Rockwell, rowing always manfully, had great difficulty in the rising sea and wind. Fortunately he realized only at rare moments the dangers of our situation.

We were now rowing continually at right angles to our true course. I had but one hope, to get to windward before the rising sea and gale overpowered us and carried us onto the dreaded coast that offered absolutely no hope. Once to windward I had the choice of making a landing in some cove or continuing for Fox Island by running with the wind astern. At last the surface of the water was fairly seething under the advancing squalls; the spray was whipped into vapor and the caldron boiled. I bent my back to the oars and put every ounce of strength into holding my own with the gale. It was a terrible moment for I saw clearly the alternative of continuing and winning our fight.

"Father," pipes up Rockwell from behind me at this tragic instant "when I wake up in the morning sometimes I pretend my toes are asleep, and I make my big toe sit up first because he's the father toe." At another time Rockwell, who had shown a little panic—a very little—said: "You know I want to be a sailor so I'll learn not to be afraid."

At last we turned and made for the island. We had reached the point where with good chances of success we could turn,—and where we had to. We reached the shelter of the island incredibly fast, it seemed, with the sea boiling in our wake, racing furiously as if to engulf us,—and then bearing us so smoothly and swiftly upon its crest that if it had not been so terrible it would have been the most soothing and delightful motion in the world. In rounding the headland of our cove a last furious effort of the eluded storm careened us sailless as we were far on one side and

The Snow Queen

carried us broadside toward the rocks. It was a minute before we could straighten our boat into the wind and pull away from the shore, then twenty feet away. Olson awaited us on the beach with tackle in readiness to haul our boat out of the surf. We landed in safety. Looking at my watch I found it to be a quarter to six. (The last four miles had taken us three hours!)

Olson's dory had been hauled up onto the grass and tied down securely. Mine was soon beside it. The tides and heavy seas of this time of year make every precaution necessary.

The wind that night continued rising till it blew a gale. And that night in their bed Rockwell and his father put their arms tight about each other without telling why they did it.

Wednesday, September Twenty-fifth

It stormed from the northeast throughout the day. After putting the cabin in order and hanging out our bedding to dry by the stove—for we had found it very damp—I set about cutting a large spruce tree whose high top shut out the light from our main windows. A few more still stand in the way. The removal of all of them should give us a fair amount of light even in the winter when the sun is hid. It occurs to me that it may be rather fortunate that my studio window looks to the south. I'll certainly not be troubled with sunlight while I may yet borrow some of the near-sun brilliancy from above our mountain's top. Rockwell and I worked some time with the cross-cut saw. I'm constantly surprised by his strength and stamina. Rockwell read nine pages in his book of the cave dwellers. So nine of "Robinson Crusoe" were due him after supper. He undresses and jumps into bed and cuddles close to me as I sit there beside him reading. And "Robinson Crusoe" is a story to grip his young fancy and make this very island a place for adventure.

Thursday, September Twenty-sixth

These are typical days, I begin to feel sure, of prevailing Alaska weather. It rains, not hard but almost constantly. Nothing is dry but the stove and the wall behind it; the vegetation is saturated, the deep moss floor of the woods is full as a sponge can be. We took the moss that weeks ago we'd gathered and spread along the shore to dry and commenced with this sopping stuff the calking of our cabin. It went rapidly and the two gable ends are nearly done. What a difference it makes; to-night when my fire roared for the biscuit baking the heat was almost unbearable. The usual chores of wood and water; a little work at manufacturing stationery; supper of farina, corn bread, peanut butter, and tea; six pages for Rockwell; and the day, but for this diary, is done.

Friday, September Twenty-seventh

At last it's fair after a clear moonlit night. I worked all day about the cabin calking it and almost finishing that job, splitting wood, and working with the cross-cut saw. Added stops to the frame of our door, made a miter box, and cut my long strips brought from Seward last trip into pieces for my stretcher frames. And Rockwell all this time helped cheerfully when he was called upon, played boat on the beach, hunted imaginary wild animals with his bow and arrow of stone-age design, and was as always so contented, so happy that the day was not half long enough.

Ah, the evenings are beautiful here and the early mornings, when the days are fair! No sudden springing of the sun into the sky and out again at night; but so gradual, so circuitous a coming and a going that nearly the whole day is twilight and the quiet rose color of morning and evening seems almost to meet at noon. We glance through our tiny western window at sunrise and see beyond the bay the many ranges of mountains, from the somber ones at the water's edge to the distant glacier and snow-capped peaks, lit by the far-off sun with the loveliest light imaginable.

To-night for supper a dish of Olson's goat's milk "Klabber" (phonetic spelling), simply sour milk with all its cream upon it, thick to a jelly. It was, in the favorite expression of Rockwell, "delicious."

Saturday, September Twenty-eighth

Beginning fresh but overcast the day soon brought us rain,—and it is now raining gently as I write. And yet we accomplished a great deal, clearing of undergrowth a part of the woods between us and the shore, felling three more trees, and cutting up a monster tree with the crosscut saw. At dinner time Olson ran in with the greatest excitement. On the path in the woods near the outlet of the lake he had seen at one time five otters. They came from the water and advanced to within twenty feet of where he and Nanny—the milk goat—stood. And there they played long enough for him to have taken a dozen pictures. In the afternoon we saw a number of otters at another place, on the rocks at one end of the beach. They were in and out of the water, going at times for little excursion swims far out into the

24

Fox Island, Resurrection Bay, Kenai Peninsula, Alaska

rocks at one end of the beach. They were in and out of the water, going at times for little excursion swims far out into the harbor, then chasing each other back and playing hide and go seek among the rocks. — This afternoon I prepared all my wood panels to begin my work, painting them on both sides.

Sunday, September 29th. — Fox Island

The Lord must have been pleased with us today for the grand cleaning up we gave this place of his. Olsen has begun to work toward me in clearing the still wild part of the intervening space between our cabins. It begins to look park like

harbor, then chasing each other back and playing hide-and-go-seek among the rocks. This afternoon I prepared all my wood panels to begin my work, painting them on both sides.

Sunday, September Twenty-ninth

The Lord must have been pleased with us to-day for the grand clearing up we gave this place of His. Olson has begun to work toward me in clearing the still wild part of the intervening space between our cabins. It begins to look parklike with trees stripped of limbs ten or twelve feet from the ground and the mossy floor beneath swept clean. With the cross-cut saw I finished up the giant tree we felled a few days ago; and then, the ground being clear, I cut the large tree that kept so much light from our windows. The difference it has made is wonderful; our room is flooded with light.

There is a fascination in cutting trees. Once I have gripped my axe, or even the tedious saw, I find it hard to relinquish it, returning to it again and again for one more cut. I believe that the clearing of homesteads gave the pioneer a compelling interest in life that was in wonderful contrast to the ordinary humdrum labor to which at first he must have been bred. It is easy to understand the rapid conquest of the wilderness; begin it— and you cannot stop.

Rockwell has set his heart upon trapping, in the kindest and most considerate way known, some wild thing—and having it for a pet. I rather discouraged his taming the sea urchin and persuaded him out of consideration for the intelligent creature's feelings to restore him to the salt water—and let me have back the bread pan. But now one of Olson's box traps is set for a magpie. They're plentiful here. I built myself a fine easel to-day, the best one I've ever had; and put a shelf under my drawing table. The room is clean and neat to-night; it is in every way a congenial place. I don't see why people need better homes than this. It was cloudy most of to-day and rained a very little from time to time. Soon I can no longer keep from painting.

Monday, September Thirtieth

The morning brilliant, clear, and cold with the wind in the north. I promised Rockwell an excursion when we had cut six sections from a tree with the cross-cut saw. It went like the wind. Then with cheese, chocolate, and Swedish hard bread in my pocket for a lunch we started for the lowest

27

Rain Torrents

ridge of the island that overlooks the east. We had always believed this to be a short and easy ascent until one day just before supper we tried it in a forced march and found, after the greatest exertions in climbing, that the ridge lay still the good part of an hour's climb above us.

So to-day, though we chose our path more wisely, it proved hard climbing along rough stream beds, across innumerable fallen trees, through alder, bramble, and blueberry thickets, and always with the soft, oozy moss underfoot. But we reached the top—steep to the very edge. Suddenly the trees ended, the land ended,—falling sheer away four hundred feet below us; and we stood in wonder looking down and out over a smooth green floor of sea and a fairyland of mountains, peaks and gorges, and headlands that cast long purple shadows on the green water. Clouds wreathed the mountains, snow was on their tops, and in the clear atmosphere both the land and the sea were marvelous for the beauty of their infinite detail. Tiny white crested wavelets patterned the water's surface with the utmost precision and regularity; and the land invited one to its smooth and mossy slopes, its dark enchanted forests, its still coves and sheltered valleys, its nobly proportioned peaks. It was a rare hour for us two.

We then followed the ridge toward the south walking in the smoothly trodden paths of the porcupines. It led us up the lofty hill on the east side of the island between its two coves. But the steepness of the ascent and the matted thickets of storm-dwarfed alders that were in our way were too much, I thought, for Rockwell, and after going some distance farther alone I returned to him and we started homewards.

Once on the mountain side we sat down in the moss and mountain cranberry to rest. And all at once we saw a great old porcupine come clambering up the hill a short way from us. I spoke to him in his own whiny-moany language and he was much pleased; he sat up, listened, and then came almost straight toward us. I continued talking to him until after several corrections of his course—determined upon by sitting up and listening—he arrived within four or five feet of Rockwell, and sat up again.

We could hardly keep from laughing, he looked so foolish. But he sensed things to be wrong, dropped down, elevated his quills, then turned and started off. Somehow I couldn't let him go without annoying him; so, grabbing a stick I pursued him poking at him to collect a few quills. But at this Rockwell set up such a shrieking and wailing that I had to stop,—and finally apologized profusely and explained that I meant no

Monday September 30th.   Fox Island.

The morning brilliant, clear and cold with the wind in the North. I promised Rockwell an excursion when we had cut six sections from a tree with the cross cut saw. It was like the wind. Then with cheese, chocolate and Swedish hard bread in my pocket for a lunch we started for the summit of the island

hard bread.
brown, brittle
and very thin.

that overlooks the east. We had always likened this to be a short and easy ascent until one day just before supper we found it in a need morsel and found, after the greatest experience in climbing that the ridge lay still the good part of an hours climb above us. So to-day, though we chose our path more wisely, it proved hard climbing along rough stream ways, across innumerable fallen trees, through alders, and brush and blueberry thickets, and always with the soft oozy moss under foot

harm to the sweet creature. Rockwell madly loves wild animals, has not the slightest fear of them, and would really, I believe, try out his theory of calming the anger of a bear by kissing him.

Then we came home and had a good dinner. I cut more wood and at last, after one month here on the island, I PAINTED. It was a stupid sketch, but no matter, I've begun! A weasel came out and looked at me as I worked, then whisked off. The magpies look into our trap, squint at the food, and then at once leave that neighborhood. It is cloudy and rainlike to-night. Is it too much to hope for more than one fair day?

III. CHORES

Tuesday, October first.—To-day it rained! We attended first to our fascinating chores, plying the cross-cut saw as the drizzle fell. Then we went to work as artists, Rockwell with his water colors and I with my oils. Rockwell has a number of good drawings of the country here and of the things that have thrilled him.

Pop! The cork of my jug of new made yeast has just struck the ceiling. That brew has been a part of this day's work. Hops, potatoes, flour, sugar, raisins, and yeast; stewed and strained and bottled. To-day also was completed and served the first

Fox Island Corn Soufflé

"Take two cups of samp (whole hominy) and stew for an indefinite time in salted water (it should cook at least three or four hours). It should boil almost dry. Make of the remainder of the water and some milk two cups of cream sauce dissolving in it some cheese. Mix with the corn and pour into a baking dish. Spread cheese over the top and put into oven to brown."

We offer this delicious discovery to the world on the condition only that "Fox Island Corn Soufflé" shall be printed on the menu wherever it is used.

31

Day

I made to-day a grandfather's chair for myself. It is as comfortable as it is beautiful.

Every day I read in the "History of Irish Literature." The Deirdre Saga I read to-day. It must be one of the most beautiful and the most perfect stories in all the world. So little do we feel ourselves related, here in this place, to any one time or to any civilization that at a thought we and our world become whom and what we please. Rockwell has been a cave dweller hunting the primeval forest with stone hatchet and a bow of alder strung with a root. To me it is the heroic age in Ireland.

WEDNESDAY, OCTOBER SECOND

Incessant, hard rain. The two artists at their work a good part of the day, Rockwell making several new drawings in his book of wonderful animals. We bathed and I washed the accumulated clothes of several weeks. And to-night Olson came for a long call. He's a good story teller and his experiences are without end. And so closes this day—with the rain still pouring monotonously on the roof.

THURSDAY, OCTOBER THIRD

To-day was fair at sunrise, cloudy at nine o'clock, and showery all the rest. We worked again with the beloved cross-cut saw, setting ourselves an almost unattainable task—and then surpassing it. And I cleared the thicket for a better view of the mountain to the south; and in the afternoon felled another large tree. Stretched canvas for a while; and painted and drew, and felt the goddess Inspiration returning to me.

Olson, Rockwell, and I, with levers and blocks, turned and emptied

Night

the three boats that the recent rains had almost filled. Already we fear the frost. The mountains have been capped with snow, all green has gone from their sides; the dark season is near at hand.

Rockwell is ever sweet, industrious, and happy. He is beautiful after his bath.

Friday, October Fourth

A gloriously lovely day, a cloudless sky and the wind in the north. That puts life into men! Up at sunrise, we two. Before breakfast the axe was going, and afterwards we brought down two mighty trees. (The trees of this part of Alaska are not to be compared with the giants of the Western States. Two feet is a large diameter.) Then I painted for a while futilely, the green and wind blown sea, the pink mountains, snowy peaks, and golden morning sky.

Rockwell and I couldn't restrain our spirits and had to clamber up the steep mountain side; up, up we went straight above our clearings; and soon, in looking back, the bay, the lake, and our neck of land lay like a map below us. Cliffs and the steep slopes baffled us at times but we found a way at last to reach the peak of the spur above us. There it was like a pavilion, a round knoll carpeted with moss, a ring of slender, clean-trunked trees; and beyond that nothing nearer than the sea nine hundred feet below. Coming down we ran across a porcupine toiling up the slope. We played with him a bit and finally let him climb a tree. Olson would have had us bring him home for dinner. They're said to taste good.

We cut with the saw a while in the afternoon. Rockwell drew and I made two more sketches, one a good one. The evening at sun-down was more brilliant even than the day. For such days as this we have come to Alaska!

Saturday, October Fifth

A hard day full of little bits of work. Sawed up a tree alone,—to punish Rockwell! for not studying. Calking the east side of the cabin—the last side. Painted, baked, and built myself an arrangement out-of-doors to sketch in comfort. I sit on the board with my palette—a box end—secured before me and my picture above it. Rockwell took his punishment so to heart that in the afternoon he read ten pages in his book. All of to-day has been overcast, but with a clean, refreshing atmosphere. In the account of Anson's voyage around the Horn it is remarked that fair weather in those latitudes rarely lasts. It may be true of the same latitudes north.

Yesterday I wrote nothing in the diary—there was nothing to write, but that it rained. "Rain like Hell" Olson's journal doubtless reads,—and ditto for to-day.

The storm is even harder now. The wind strikes our cabin first from the west, then north, east, and south. The surface of the cove is seething under the cross squalls; that is called the "wullys." A boat not strongly managed would be whipped round and round. Olson has been much in to see us, lonely old man! I drop my drawing while he is here and take to stretching canvas, all the while yarning with him. Rockwell likes the calls as a diversion. Rockwell's good humor and contentment is without limit.

Rockwell drew and I made two more sketches — me a good one. The evening at Sundown was more brilliant even than the day. For such days as this we have come to Alaska!

Saturday, October 5th, 1918, Fox Island.
A hard day free of little bits of work. Sawed up a tree alone — to punish Rockwell! for not studying

He draws with the deepest interest hours a day, reads for a time, and plays—talking to himself.

We have good hearty fights together in which Rockwell attacks me with all his strength and I hit back with force in self-defense. We have a good time washing dishes, racing,—the washer, myself, to beat the dryer. Rockwell falls down onto the floor in the midst of the race in a fit of laughter. Rockwell's happiness is not complete until I spank him. I grab the struggling creature and throw him down, trying to hold both his hands and feet to have free play in beating him. This I do with some strength sometimes using a stick of kindling wood. The more it hurts the better Rockwell likes it—up to a limit that we never reach.

So much for the day's play. Of our work mine is mostly over the drawing table. Both yesterday and to-day I made good drawings; and my ideas come crowding along fast. Cooking, somehow, is the least troublesome of all the daily chores. We live, as may be imagined, with a simplicity that would send a Hoover delegate flying from the door in dismay. This is our daily fare:

BREAKFAST
(invariably the same)
Oatmeal, Cocoa
Bread and Peanut Butter

DINNER
Beans (one of several kinds and several ways)
or Fox Island Corn Soufflé
or Spaghetti or Peas
or Vegetable Stew
(barley, carrots, potatoes)
and Potatoes or rice
and (often)
Prunes or apricots or apples (dried)

SUPPER
(invariably the same)
Farina
Corn bread with peanut butter or marmelade
Tea for father, milk for son
And sometimes dessert—stewed fruit, chocolate,
or, when Olson gives it, goat milk junket.

Let us here record that to this date we have had not the least little sickness,—only glowing health and good spirits.

Tuesday, October Eighth

RAIN! But what difference does it make to us. Everyone is in a good humor. The house is warm and dry; we've lots to eat and lots to do.

Olson's dory was again half full of water so we turned her and the skiff over. I stretched canvas and primed it and finished Anson's "Voyage Around the World" a thrilling book. Late this afternoon it began to clear; the sun shone and we were presently at work with the saw—only to be driven in again by the shower. I expect fair weather to-morrow. But—

Wednesday, October Ninth

Fair weather is still as far away as ever, unless a sharp but cloudy afternoon and sundown with brilliant light in the western sky spell change. Olson says the foxes will not eat to-night and that this is invariably a sign of change to good days—that in bad weather they eat and in fair they abstain. It poured in the morning and we worked indoors. After dinner we all moved a lumber pile that stood on the shore abreast of our cabin to a place nearer Olson's—this only to better our view of the water. We sawed wood for a while and piled all that we have so far cut ready for

38

Wilderness

One of Rockwell's Drawings

winter use. There are in all fifty sections of short stove wood. That is a month and a half's supply. I painted towards evening, and made two good sketches.

The nights have grown colder. For the past two days the mountains across from us, the nearest ones, have been covered with snow downwards to half their height. The farther ranges have for weeks been white. They're beautiful and invite one to go climbing and sliding over their smooth white snowfields. Close to, one would find impassable crags and crevasses, a howling wind and bitter cold. Rockwell to-day finished his second book, "The Cave Dwellers."

Midnight Bulletin: the stars are out, brilliant in a cloudless sky!

THURSDAY, OCTOBER TENTH

It's raining! All day has been overcast, but sharp and clear. It was for us all a day of hard work. We cleared up the woods between Olson's cabin and ours carrying one large pile of brush from our door yard to the beach and burning another huge one. That was a wild sight as night came. It

40

had become a great fire of logs burning steadily and lighting up all the woods around. It is still burning in the pouring rain. We sawed a little—always more than keeping pace with our consumption of wood. Rockwell worked almost the whole day and went to bed tired. I read to him an hour. He loves to hear poetry.

We set an elaborate contrivance to catch a magpie; and were humiliated by the bird who walked round and round the snare eying it wisely, then suddenly rushed in only far enough to secure a piece of decoy bait—and fled. Painted to-day making a good little sketch, but, on my first trial of the home-made canvas, finding it to need more priming. Work! work!

Friday, October Eleventh

This day we should have been in Seward. It was calm although it rained from time to time. Olson offered to tow us across to Caine's Head; but, the rain coming up as we were about to start in the morning, we waited till afternoon, started, proceeded half a mile, encountered engine trouble, and finally ignominiously rowed home, I pulling Olson and his motor and Rockwell bringing in our own dory. If it had not been so late we would have kept on.

We have a magpie. I saw one hop into Olson's shed, quickly ran and closed the door, and there he was. Now he's in a box-trap cage on a specially constructed shelf on our front gable. He's a garrulous creature and bites angrily; but he's a youngster and we hope to teach him to say all sorts of pretty things; Olson says they take naturally to swearing. So Rockwell has at last a pet.

If only it will hold calm! To-night it is fair and star-light—but we can never be sure of the weather's constancy. We hold everything in readiness to start in the morning.

Saturday, October Twelfth

A mild and lovely day on our island but in the bay a breeze from the north that would have made our rowing to Seward difficult. Still we wait with our things assembled for the trip. We shall go at the very first good chance. This morning Olson cleared the limbs from the trees about us to ten or twelve feet from the ground. Only the tall, clean trunks are now between us and our mountains across the bay. I painted most of the afternoon. My canvas is still quite impossible—rough and absorbent. We built a large cage for the magpie he was so restless in his small one. And now he's quite contented.

is still quite impossible rough and disordant. He built a large cage for the Magpie, he was so restless in his small one. And now he's quite contented

Rockwell said to-day that he would like to live here always. That when he was grown he'd come here with his many children and me, if I was not dead, and stay. — It is hard to write, it is hard to work, with the trip to Seward at hand. Olson says it is Sunday. I think he's right. Somehow I've missed a day.

42

Rockwell said to-day that he would like to live here always. That when he was grown he'd come here with his many children and me, if I was not dead, and stay. It is hard to write, it is hard to work, with the trip to Seward at hand. Olson says it is Sunday. I think he's right. Somehow I've missed a day.

Sunday, October Thirteenth

(I still keep to my chronology until we find out from Seward where we stand.) A wonderfully beautiful day with a raging northwest wind. I must sometime honor the northwest wind in a great picture as the embodiment of clean, strong, exuberant life, the joy of every young thing, bearing energy on its wings and the will to triumph. How I remember at Monhegan on such a day, when it seemed that every living thing must emerge from its house or its hole or its nest to breathe the clean air and exult in it; when men could stand on the hilltops and look far over the green sea and the distant land and delight in the infinite detail of the view, discerning distant ships at sea and remote blue islands, and, over the land, sparkling cities and such enchanting forests and pastures that the spirit leaped the intervening miles and with a new delight claimed the whole earth to the farthest mountains—and beyond; on such a day there crept from his hole an artist, and, shading his squinting eyes with his hand, saluted the day with a groan. "How can one paint?" he said, "such sharpness! Here is no mystery, no beauty." And he crept back, this fog lover, to wait for earth's sick spell to return.

This morning the magpie sang—or recited poetry; he made strange glad noises in his throat—and that in a cage! We worked, the rest of us, like mad. At five-thirty Olson, resting at last, said: "Well, you've done a great day's work." And after that I painted a sketch, cut and trimmed three small spruce trees; and then, it being dark, prepared supper.

But when do we go to Seward? My bag is packed. Olson begins each day by testing his motor. The wind must moderate in time. We see it pass our cove driving the water as in a mill-race. To-day it swept the cove itself.

Rockwell went for a walk in the woods; he has a delightful time on his rambles, discovering goat's wool on the bushes, following the paths of the porcupines to their holes, and to-day finding the porcupine himself. He always returns with some marvelous discovery or new enthusiasm

43

Sunrise

over his explorations. He has been practicing writing to-day. He says that if he could only write he would put down the wonderful stories of his dreams. These stories would run into volumes.

Yesterday we left the island. The day was calm though cloudy, and at times it rained. Olson towed us to Caine's Head. From there we made good time Rockwell rowing like a seasoned oarsman, as indeed he has now a right to be called. We stopped at the camp where we had in August left our broken-down engine, and brought that away with us, as well as some turnips and half a dozen heads of beautiful lettuce grown on that spot.

By night it was raining hard and blowing from the southeast. We spent the evening at the postmaster's house, playing, I, on the flute to Miss Postmaster's accompaniment. It went splendidly and until midnight we played Beethoven, Bach, Haydn, Gluck, Tchaikowsky, till it seemed like old times at home. Then Rockwell with his eyes shut in sleep, consumed a piece of apricot pie and a glass of milk, and we came home bringing along two glasses of wild currant preserve. I read my letters over and then went to bed. But the storm raged by that time and I couldn't sleep for worry about my boat. At last I rose and dressed and went down to the shore. The dory was safely stranded but too low down. So with great toil I worked her higher up the beach beyond high water.

To-day it has rained incessantly. I have bought a few odd supplies and registered for the draft.

Above all to-day the engine has resumed its running and we'll return to Fox Island under power. I know nothing about an engine but I have eight miles to learn in before the only hazardous part of the voyage begins. To-night Rockwell and I spent the evening at the house of a young man whom we've found congenial and who above all is a friend of a young German mechanic for whom I've a liking. So the four of us sang the evening through, seated before a great open fire. The house is of logs and stands out of the town on the border of the wilderness. There are spots like this little house and its hospitable hearth that show even the commercial desert of Seward to have its oases. And now we're in our room. Rockwell is asleep in bed. It is past midnight. I am thinking of dear friends at home, and I bid them affectionately good-night.

Adventure

46

Thursday, October Seventeenth

Yesterday in Seward was about as every other day. We spent it between letter-writing in our hotel room and visiting from store to store. It poured rain and blew from the southeast. We spent our evening with the German. We have planned with him to signal back and forth from Seward, particularly to send me the news of peace. If I can distinguish, with glasses, a high-powered electric light that he will show from a house on the highest point in the town, then, by means of the Morse code with which I am furnished and which he knows, I'll receive messages on appointed days.

To-night Rockwell and I went a quarter of a mile down our beach to a point that commands a view up the bay to Seward and lighted a bonfire there. Boehm, the German, was regarding us, we presume, through a telescope. On Sunday night, if it is clear, we are to look for his light. The difficulty will be to distinguish it from others.

We left Seward this morning at 9:45, our dory laden with about one thousand pounds of freight—including ourselves. The little three and one half horse-power motor worked splendidly and carried us to the island in a little over two and a quarter hours. The day was calm, to begin with, with a rising north wind as we crossed from Caine's Head. On the island we found a visitor. There had been two other men but they were gone to Seward the night before. All had been on Monday forced by the rough sea to turn back from attempting to go around the westward cape. The old fellow who is still here told me to-night that in the twenty years that he had been in Alaska he had never seen such weather. That's good news. At Seward the mountains are covered with snow to within a few hundred feet of the town's level. I'm tired. This ends to-day. Incidentally my dates proved to be correct when I reached Seward.

Oh, I've almost forgotten our loss. The poor magpie lay dead on the floor of his cage. So we found him, killed, I believe, by the storm, for Olson neglected to cover him. Rockwell, who straight on landing had run there, wept bitterly but finally found much consolation in giving him a very decent burial and marking the spot with a wooden cross.

FRIDAY, OCTOBER EIGHTEENTH

"Guter Mond, du gehst so stille
Durch die Abend Wolken hin."

The night is beautiful beyond thought. All the bay is flooded with moon-light and in that pale glow the snowy mountains appear whiter than snow itself. The full moon is almost straight above us, and shining through the tree tops into our clearing makes the old stumps quite lovely with its quiet light. And the forest around is as black as the abyss. Although it is nearly ten o'clock Rockwell is still awake. It is his birthday—by our choice. His one present, a cheap child's edition of Wood's "Natural History," illus-trated, has filled his head with dreams of his beloved wild animals. I began to-night to teach him to sing. We tried Brahms' "Wiegenlied," with little success, and then "Schlaf, Kindlein, Schlaf," which went better. These songs and many other German songs, all with English words, are in the song book I bought him. I hope I shall have the patience and the time to succeed with Rockwell in this.

Three men are now with Olson in his cabin, for the two who were gone to Seward returned to-day. They are younger men, one of them Emsweiler a well-known guide of this country. I spent an interesting hour with them this evening. Olson told me to-day that his age is seventy-one. The smell of fresh bread is in our cabin, for I baked to-day. Baking, wood-cutting, darning of socks, putting the cabin in order, and the building of a shelf, these, with the other usual chores, were the whole day's work; a profitless day lies on my conscience. I shall draw a little and then go to bed.

Immediately my dates proved to be correct
when I reached Seward.

Oh, I've almost forgotten our loss.
The poor magpie lay dead on the floor
of his cage. So we found him.
Killed, I believe, by the storm - for
Olsen neglected to cover him. Rockwell,
who, straight on landing, had seen these
things verbally had finally found much
consolation in giving him a very decent
burial and marking the spot with a
wooden cross.

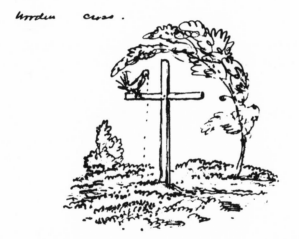

Friday October 18th. Fox Island.

"Guter Mond, du gehst so stille
Durch die Abend Wolken hin."

The night is beautiful beyond thought.
All the bay is flooded with moonlight
and in that pale light the snowy

49

Saturday, October Nineteenth

To-day was raw and cloudy, mild and sunny; in the morning windy, in the afternoon dead calm so that the hills were reflected in the bay. The men have left, I am glad to say, not that they were in themselves at all objectionable, but it somehow did violence to the quiet of this place to have others about. Emsweiler slaughtered one of the goats for Olson, so there's now one less of us here. I felled a large tree to-day and later sharpened the cross-cut saw preparatory to cutting it up. To-night the sun set in the utmost splendor and left in its wake blazing, fire-red clouds in a sky of luminous green. Not many more days shall we see the sun; it sets now close to the southern headland of our cove.

Rockwell works every day on his wild animal book. To obtain absolutely new and original names for his strange creatures he has devised an interesting method. With eyes closed he prints a name or rather a group of miscellaneous letters. Naturally the result he perceives on opening his eyes is astonishing.

Sunday, October Twentieth

It has been a beautiful, clear, cold, violent northwest day. I've painted on and off all day, with wood cutting between. One can't stop going in such weather, and out-of-doors you can't stand still for it is too icy cold and windy.

Rockwell and I have just now, eight o'clock, returned from down the beach where we went to look for lights from Seward. But we could distinguish nothing meant for us. The moon has risen and illuminates the mountain tops—but we and all our cove are still in the deep shadow of the night. It is most dramatic; the spruces about us deepen the shadow to black while above them the stone faces of the mountain glisten and the sky has the brightness of a kind of day. Olson brought us goat chops for dinner. We could not have told them from lamb.

This afternoon late a small power boat appeared in the bay attempting to make its way toward Seward. After some progress the wind forced her steadily and swiftly back. When we last saw her she seemed to be trying to make the shelter of our island or one of the outer islands, the while driving steadily seaward. It's a wild night to be out in the bay though doubtless calm at sea. It is such an adventure that we must be on our guard against. As we look across the bay toward Bear Glacier, which is hidden by a point of land, we can see the effect of the north wind sweep-

felled a large tree to-day and later sharpened the cross-cut saw preparatory to cutting it up. To-night the sun set in the utmost splendor and left in its wake flaming fire-red clouds in a sky of luminous green. Not many more days shall we see the sun; it sets now close to the Southwest head-land of our cove

This is the sky-line of the island to the south. It is these mountains that hide the sun from us. Rockwell works every day on his wild animal book. To obtain absolutely new and original names for his strange creatures he has devised an interesting method. With eyes closed he prints a name or perhaps rather a group of miscellaneous letters. Naturally

51

ing down the glacier, a mist driving seaward. It is nothing less than the fine spray of that wind-swept water.

Monday, October Twenty-first

It is so late that I shall write only a little. To-day was again wonderful, a true golden and blue northwest day. I have painted and sawed wood, and built myself a splendid six-legged saw horse. Olson thinks I have already cut my winter's supply of wood—but it seems to me far from it. Rockwell has been most of the day at his own animal book, making some strange and beautiful birds. This morning the ground was frozen with a hard crust. It did not thaw throughout the day, and again to-night it is very cold. Winter is at last upon us, the long, long winter. And the sun retreats day by day farther toward the mountain. I look to the sun's going with a kind of dread. We have seen nothing of the boat that last night was driven to shelter. We believe the men to be in the other cove of our island.

Tuesday, October 22nd. Fox Island

The day has gone in hard work, the final tuning up for winter. And here it is upon us, for the snow is falling. We sawed a week's wood and stacked the drums; caulked the cabin under the eaves with hemp; set up the new stove, carrying the pipe out through the roof and securing it in good workmanlike fashion; repaired the roof in some places—though it must, I fear, continue in the hard storms to filter water through it; piled two sides of the cabin, on the outside, high with brush. Our cabin is now far more comfortable than Olson's and we are ever so much better prepared for the winter. Rockwell's help has counted a great deal. He has grown very much this fall,—Olson remarked it tonight,—and can in some things almost do a man's work. He's untiring at his end of the cross-cut saw. The day has been grey, cold and windy,—but it's grand weather for hard work.

Wednesday, October 23rd. Fox Island

Now that stupid old Robinson Crusoe has been laid aside—with a dozen or so pages still unread—and "Treasure Island" begun, the entries in my diary must be short. But the evenings are noticeably longer. We have no exact way of knowing when we get up or go to bed. Our time piece is a dollar Ingersoll that, when worn out by its original owner, was given to Olson. He shook it, on and off, for a year more till it would give him no

have told them from land. This afternoon late a small power boat appeared in the bay attempting to make its way toward Seward. After some progress the wind forced her steadily and swiftly back. When we last saw her she seemed to be trying to make the shelter of an island or one of the outer islands, the while driving steadily seaward. It's a wild night to be out, though doubtless calm at sea. It is such an adventure that we must be on our guard against. As we look across the bay toward Bear glacier, which is hidden by a point of land. we can see the effect of the north wind sweeping down the glacier in a mist driving toward the sea. It is nothing less than the fine spray of that wind-swept water.

I finished to-day "the Literary History of Ireland" that Carl gave me. It might do the public some good to learn, as one does in this work, that there _is_ ground for German-Irish friendship, in that German scholars stand almost alone in the respect in which they have held Irish civilization and in the study they have given its records. — The day has been beautiful. The slight fall of snow from last night still lies upon the ground and over the across-the-water mountains like a gray veil. And the wind that all day blew now rages.

more service, and then passed it on to Rockwell. Dipped in kerosene it runs, certainly, but raggedly. But I am under the impression that the sun rises between half past seven and eight, and sets before six. But after setting it is for a long time light in the west. We have at any rate almost come to the average winter day. And as for temperature—am I to believe Olson? He came to our cabin this morning looking very cold. "Well," he cries, "how does the winter suit you?" It was then, I should judge, about 25, yet he says it's a typical winter day and calls it cold! I suspect frozen Alaska to be just such a myth as fog and snow bound Newfoundland.—After the morning's wood cutting I worked hard on my pictures. I'm now at last fully launched upon my work with small pictures going well. That's both a relief and a concern to me. From now on my mind can never be quite free. Rockwell and I took a short walk in the woods after dinner skirting the lake. From the southern end I was surprised to see the mountains east of the island standing up above us, so near, it seemed, that a stranger might have thought of climbing them in one hour's time.

I finished today "The Literary History of Ireland" that Carl gave me. It might do the public some good to learn, as one does in this work, that there is ground for German-Irish friendship, in that German scholars stand almost alone in the respect in which they have held Irish civilization and in the study they have given its records.—The day has been beautiful. The slight fall of snow from last night still lies upon the ground and over the across-the-water mountains like a gray veil. And the wind that all day blew now rages.

Fox Island, October 24th. Thursday

This creature, the "air-tight," is the greatest comfort imaginable. We pile it full of chunks of wood of every size and then forget it, all but the steady warmth that is regulated by the damper. Filled with wood it will smoulder the night through and burst again into flame at the opening of the draught. We cook on it too when it is more convenient.—Today was a day of hard work for me. I cut wood, baked bread and painted on three canvasses. Over to-day's painting I'm filled with pride; it will be equalled by to-morrow's despair over the very same pictures. Olson called upon me today to perform a surgical operation on one of the foxes. It was a lump the size of an egg on the beast's "elbow." Olson held the fox while I made a cut two inches long and took out a mass of fat and gristle. I pronounced it a fatty tumor. The fox, after his first paroxysms at being

Tor Island, October, 24th, Thursday.

This creature, the "air-tight" is the greatest comfort imaginable. The pile is full of chunks of wood of every size and then forget it all but the steady warmth that is regulated by the dampers. Filled with wood it will smoulder the night through and burst again into flames at the opening of the draught. The cork on is too when it is more convenient. — To-day was a day of hard work — for me. I cut wood baked bread and painted on three canvasses. One to-days painting I'm filled with pride; it will be equalled

56

caught, minded it not a bit.—We had today "Fox Island Corn Souffle." It was as usual a complete success. And so was the bread. The hop yeast works wonderfully.—Today was again most beautiful. At sunset it grew milder and the look of coming snow, but now, at a late hour, the wind is again strong from the North. Olson has already waited many days for a chance to go to Seward. It is a hazardous trip in the winter time for the interminable loss of time and the expense it is apt to occasion by one's being held, possibly for weeks, in Seward.

Friday, October 25th. Fox Island

It has all day been cloudy and windy but less cold. Last night the moon threw a great circle of light in the sky, and that should portend a storm. We've wood in the house and all that we have cut out of doors is securely piled. I worked today on a linoleum block introductory to wood cutting; and I painted as well—with some success. Rockwell drew for hours on a chart of an imaginary island. It is most interesting.

Saturday, October 26th. Fox Island

A miserable day, storming violently and snowing, and, worst of all, nothing accomplished. The men are still here on the island. A trip along the beach to the other cove disclosed the fact that the missing boat is not there. They now believe her to have been stolen by some of the crew of a disabled schooner that put into Seward some weeks ago.

Sunday, October 27th. Fox Island

A cheerless day, not cold but damp and chilly with clouds overhead and occasional rain falling. The two visitors left the island early this morning though it was blowing rather stiffly. They aimed to reach Seward by the east shore of the bay. I have been all day cutting stretchers and stretching and painting the canvas—and I have but four done. These still must have a second coat. Rockwell has been letter writing. It's too bad we must be taught to conform to rules in spelling. Rockwell's spelling is an analysis of the sounds he knows as words, and it's wonderfully funny. His text to the animal pictures in his book will be left uncorrected. Rockwell set the box trap today for a porcupine. He will have a pet and he has a notion that this creature can be taught to follow him about like a dog. If it does there's no doubt we'll bring him home with us.

Friday, October 25th, Fox Island.

Einsmuller, the guide, mentioned in these pages a few days back came to the island this morning with another man. They're in search of that man's boat which disappeared from Seward last Sunday. The boat we saw from here on Sunday struggling against the wind answers the description of the lost boat. Who was aboard of her? Had she been picked up adrift and was she being taken back to Seward? Or - as Einsmuller suggests - was she stolen, perhaps by men attempting to evade the draft? In any case she's still in some cove of this bay, in hiding or disabled, or she has put to sea and escaped. There is too the chance that she was wrecked Sunday night. It was too rough to-day to continue the search. The men are stopping with Olsen.

Monday, October 28th. Fox Island

A quiet, mild, gray day. Olsen should have gone to Seward, but he dallied too long. He will try it to-morrow. I have exhausted myself tonight letter writing, but after all there's little to record here. A day of painting and an uninspired one. A little wood cutting, my canvases second-coated, and that is all. Rockwell all day in wonderful spirits. He still runs about bare kneed, a fashion we've fallen into because he lacks woollen stockings. But till his knees feel the cold he shall wear my socks and incline nature perhaps to coat the knees with fur as were Rob Roy's. "Treasure Island" was finished to Rockwell two days ago and now we're upon "Water Babies." That's just after his heart—and mine too.

Tuesday, October 29th. Fox Island

Olson is at Seward! It was a dead calm today, and after one start from which the rain drove him back he got off in safety. But first this morning he shot a grouse which he brought to us. Rockwell cried bitterly over it and his true little heart made no mistake. It is a shame that for the sake of a few paltry mouthfuls the wild woods should be robbed of one of its people. Olson is a nice and good hearted man and never kills wantonly; but at best man's preying on the wild life about him is nothing short of barbarism. Rockwell's natural love for every living thing, his claim, which is half play and half a real belief, that everything that lives is his child should put us all to shame. Today I did little but paint. And for that the light was poor. On a dark day in this dark walled cabin, with the woods about and the sun itself, wherever it may be, behind the clouds, still in certainty somewhere behind the mountains, there is hardly light enough to read by except close to the window. I milked the goat tonight and mighty little she gave me. The foxes are not to be fed till the day after tomorrow,—and it looks promising for Olson's quick return. Still I have full directions for the care of all the creatures.

Squirlie is Rockwell's pet, brought from home with us. It sleeps every night close in Rockwell's (his mother's) arms. I begin to almost believe in it myself.

Wednesday, October 30th. Fox Island

It must be almost morning. We go now without any time-piece; get up at daylight or later, eat when we are hungry—tho' breakfast we have promptly enough; and after supper I read to Rockwell from ten to thirty pages,

I milked the goat to-night and might little she gave me. The foxes are not to be fed 'til the day after to-morrow. — and it looks promising for Olsen's quick return. Still I have full directions for the care of all the creatures.

This is
SQUIRLIE.

Squirlie is Rockwell's pet, brought from home with us. It sleeps every night close in Rockwell's (his mother's) arms I begin to almost believe in it my-self.

Wednesday, October 30th. Fox Island.

It must be almost morning. We go now without any time-piece; get up at daylight or later, eat when we are hungry — tho' breakfast we have

write and draw and read a bit to myself, and go to bed without any notion of the hour. Tonight I've made a number of pen and ink drawings and have at last drawn a design upon a wood block. It is a wonderful surface to draw upon. The day has passed in hard work. I have painted almost continually, the chores, even with the goat to stable and milk, seeming to have taken no time at all. Rockwell has read for hours. We both sit reading at our meals now. It's a splendid scheme to put the brakes on hungry feeders and gives me at least my only regular hours of reading. Olson could not return today; it storms heavily from the Northeast with every prospect of continuing indefinitely. Rockwell improves the opportunity to play unrestrainedly with the goats. Billy, the ram, dances threateningly on his hind legs before him to Rockwell's immense delight.

Thursday, October 31st. Fox Island

Rain and snow today. Olson still held in Seward. On such a day—particularly with Olson not here to drop in and amuse and disturb us with his talk—our cabin is a true workshop. Rockwell at one table draws, writes and reads. I work at the other, or paint. Today I spent on my first wood block. After sharpening my tools and making a new one out of a file I began work and cut all day on a block not two inches square; and it is only half done now!—It is now just past supper. On ending this writing I play the flute for Rockwell to sing by, read a chapter of "Water Babies" and then begin my night session of work.

Friday, November 1st. Fox Island

The days are now pretty much alike so far as our activities are concerned. I painted and worked at my wood block. It is now finished but I have no way of getting a good enough impression of it to judge it by. I have tried oil paint for printer's ink and it doesn't go well and I'm afraid of clogging the block in persisting in such trials. Rockwell has today devoted himself to the goats. He came in this morning in great glee to tell me that they thought he was a goat. I agreed with them when he went on to tell me how he had climbed the mountain-side with them on all fours pretending to browse and conversing with them in the goats' tongue. Sometimes the goats are a nuisance. Billy ate two mouthfulls out of our broom this morning before I caught him at it. Milked the goat and fed the foxes again today, for Olson is still away. We thought that today he should have returned. It was not too windy though it snowed on and off. It was extremely mild. Once I sent Rockwell far down the beach to look up the bay toward Seward, and a score of times I have gone to the window in the hope of seeing Olson rounding the point of our cove.

IV. WINTER

Endlessly, day after day, the journal goes on recording a dreary monotony of rain and cloud. Who has ever dwelt so entirely alone that the most living things in all the universe about are wind and rain and snow? Where the elements dominate and control your life, where at getting up and bedtime and many an hour of night and day between, you question helplessly, as a poor slave his master, the will of the mighty forces of the sky? Dawn breaks, you jump from bed, stand barefoot on the threshold of the door, look through the straight trunked spruces at the brightening world, and read at sight God's will for one more whole, long day of life. "Ah God! it rains again." And sitting on the bed you wearily draw on your heavy boots, and rainy-spirited begin the special labors of a rainy day. Or maybe, at the sight of clouds again, you laugh at the dull-minded weather man or curse at him good naturedly. Still you must do those rainy-weather chores and all the other daily chores in hot wet-weather garments. That is destiny.

Most of the time, to do ourselves real justice, we met the worst of weather with a battle cry, worked hard,—and then made up for outdoor dreariness and wet by heaping on the comforts of indoors,—dry, cozy warmth, good things to eat, and lots to do.

We have reached late fall—for northern latitudes. The sky is brooding ominously, heavy, dull, and raw. Winter seems to be closing in upon us. We're driven to work as if in fear. Hurry, hurry! Saw the great drums of spruce, roll them over the ground and stack them high. Calk tight with hemp the cabin's windward eaves so that no breath of wind can enter there and freeze the food inside upon the shelf. Set up the far-famed air-tight stove where it will keep you warm,—warm feet in bed and a warm back while painting. Patch up the poor, storm-battered paper roof,—two or three holes we find and we are sure it leaks from twenty. About the cabin pile the hemlock boughs, dense-leafed and warm, making a green slope almost to the eaves. Now it looks cozy! Outside and in, the last is done to make us ready for the winter's worst, and just in time! It is the evening of October twenty-second and the feathery snow has just begun to fall. Olson comes stamping in. "Well, well," he cries, "how's this! How does our winter suit you?" It suits us perfectly. The house is warm, Rockwell's in bed, and I am reading "Treasure Island" to him.

"What are you going to make of him?" asked Olson that night speaking of Rockwell. I was at that moment pouring beans into the pot for baking. I slowed the stream and dropped them one by one:

" 'Rich-man, poor-man, beggar-man, thief,
Doctor, lawyer, merchant, chief.'
How in the world can anyone lay plans for a youngster's life?"

Rockwell lay in his bed dreaming, maybe, of an existence lovelier far than anything the poor, discouraged imagination of a man could reach. A child could make a paradise of earth. Life is so simple! Unerringly he follows his desires making the greatest choices first, then onward into a narrowing pathway until the true goal is reached. How can one preach of beauty or teach another wisdom. These things are of an infinite nature, and in every one of us in just proportion. There is no priesthood of the truth.

We live in many worlds, Rockwell and I,—the world of the books we read,—an always changing one, "Robinson Crusoe," "Treasure Island," the visionary world of William Blake, the Saga Age, "Water Babies," and the glorious Celtic past,—Rockwell's own world of fancy, kingdom of beasts, the world he dreams about and draws,—and my created land of striding heroes and poor fatebound men—real as I have painted them or to me nothing is,—and then all round about our common daily, island-world, itself more wonderful than we have half a notion of. Is it to be believed that we are here alone, this boy and I, far north out on an island wilderness, seagirt on a terrific coast! It's as we pictured it and wanted it a year and more ago,—yes, dreams come true.

64

On the Height

And now the snow falls softly. Winter, to meet our challenge, has begun.

Short notes in the journal mark "Treasure Island's" swift passage. Then enter "Water Babies!" "Just after Rockwell's heart and mine," I have recorded it. But Kingsley must lose his friends,—a warning to the snob in literature. How it did weary us and madden us, his English-gentry pride,— unless we outright laughed. "At last it's finished. That's an event. When Kingsley isn't showing off he's moralizing, and between his religious cant and his English snobbery he is, in spite of his occasional sweet sentiment, quite unendurable. So to-night we read from 'Andersen's Fairy Tales'— forever lovely and true."

Children have their own fine literary taste that we know quite too little about. They love all real, authentic happenings, and they love pure fairy tale. But to them fiction in the guise of truth is wrong, and fairy romance, unconvincing in its details, is ridiculous. Action they like, the deed—not thoughts about it. Doubtless the simple saga form is best of all,—life as it happens, neither right nor wrong, words that they can understand, things they can comprehend, interesting facts or thrilling fancy. Such simple things delight the child that half of "Robinson Crusoe" and three quarters of the smug family from Switzerland are forgiven for the sweet kernel of pure adventure that is there.

As for adventure,—that is relative. Where little happens and the gamut of expression is narrow, life is still full of joy and sorrow. You're stirred by simple happenings in a quiet world.

The killer-whales that early in September played in the shoal water of our cove not thirty feet from land, rolled their huge, shining bodies into view, plunged, raced where we still could follow their gleaming white patch under water,—there's a thrill!

The battles that occurred that month between huge fish out in the bay, their terrible, mysterious, black arms that beat the water with a sound like cannon, the plunge into the depths of the poor, frantic, wounded whale, and his return again for air; again the thunder sound and flying foam and spray as the dread black arm is beating on the sea; then calm. You shudder at that huge death. That was a drama for Fox Islanders.

And later the poor magpie's death. Real tears were shed from a poor boy's half-broken heart.

Two strangers come these days and stop with Olson. They're on the search of that small craft that we saw driving seaward in a tempest. There

66

The Day's Work

67

is mystery! Was she adrift unmanned, broke from her moorings, or was there life aboard as we had thought? In that case she'd been stolen, and who were the men and where? Wrecked safely on some island, drowned, or driven out to sea? No man shall ever know.

A porcupine is captured wandering near our house. We build for him a cozy home—he doesn't like it much but still he should. We care for him day after day, he twines himself about our hearts. Then at last one day when we'd pastured him in freedom out in the new fallen snow, trusting his tracks to lead us to him, the goats cut in and spoiled the trail and he was lost to us.

Olson has gone to Seward: days of waiting, days of waiting! How many times do we travel down the cove to the point from whence Caine's Head is seen, going in hope, returning gloomily.

The goats beset us yearning for their missing master. Billy, that maddening beast, eats up one corner of our broom. I throw a heavy armful of kindling wood into his face—and he just sneezes. But Rockwell plays with the goats as if they're human, or rather, as if he were goat. They half believe it, he has told me,—and, Rockwell, so do I.

Sunday, November Third

To-day was gloriously bright and clear with a strong northwest wind. The mountains are covered with snow, beautiful beyond description. I painted in- and out-of-doors continuously all the day except when Rockwell and I plied the saw. It is no little thing to have one's work on a day like this out under such a blue sky, by the foaming green sea and the fairy mountains.

Sunday, November 3rd. Fox Island

Last night I finished my work at too late an hour to write in this book— and too elated to descend to prose after the fine drawing I had completed. But yesterday was as uneventful as a day could be. The wind blew, the sky was overcast and the sea was in white caps. I painted all the day till nightfall, except for a little wood cutting with Rockwell, and then at almost dark we went for a short walk along the goat paths of the woods;— and that was yesterday.

Sunday, Nov. 3rd. Fox Island (continued)

Rockwell plays with the goats, following them about and gets a lot of

68

fun from it. They all invaded my cabin today, the door chancing to be open. Goats need rough language and hard blows to make them heed you. I threw an armfull of kindling in Billy's face as he stood in the doorway and he merely sneezed. Sometimes the magpies come into the house; one did today but not far enough to be trapped. Olson is still at Seward. How long this wind will continue no one can tell. It would take a well manned dory to be out on such a day as this.

TUESDAY, NOVEMBER 5TH. FOX ISLAND

Again a two days entry. Yesterday, briefly, was mild and rainy beginning however with snow that lay as it fell on every twig and gave us for a few hours our first real picture of winter. The wind rose during the day and spoiled what might have been a good chance for Olson's return. It was so dark all day that we both breakfasted and dined by lamp light—and finally went supperless to bed.

To-day it rained and hailed a bit. It is still wild and the ice that had formed over all the lake is rapidly melting. At sea there must have been a mighty storm for the largest surf of the fall is breaking on the land across the bay. It has seemed a perfectly good chance for Olson's return but still he has not come—and the eighth day of his absence has begun. I am incessantly at work painting while there is light, and drawing otherwise. I fear the sun will no longer shine on us this winter. On the last fine day it showed but an hour at noon. We captured a small porcupine that strayed near the cabin. Rockwell is delighted with this stupid pet, though I have had to tell him that we cannot keep it. Nothing could be more unattractive than a porcupine's mangy looking back of coarse hair and quills—and his back is all he ever shows to visitors. This has been an off day for Rockwell and he cried a bit. We enter this because it is an unusual event and as a punishment to Rockwell who, it is hoped, will not care to have his lapses thus imperishably recorded. The goats are well and the foxes seemingly more tame. The tamest of them came close enough to gnaw at my hip pocket as I stooped with his food.

Three days go by. It rains and hails and snows, and then is quiet. Over the dead, still air comes the roar of pounding seas. Immense and white they pile on the black cliffs of Caine's Head, the wash of a storm at sea. Still over the heaving, glassy water we look in vain for Olson. Dark days, and the short hours are long with waiting. How many times we traveled down the cove to look toward Seward, how many score of times we peered through the little panes of our west window never to find the thing we sought for.

I've loaded my arms with firewood from the pile. I turn my head and there in our cove before my very eyes at last is Olson! This is November sixth,—nine days away!

Wednesday, November 6th. Fox Island

Olson returned this evening with news that Peace is at hand! Thank God! At the same time there would be a pitiless justice in the continuance of such a war to the extermination of all those men to whom mass bloodshed appeals as something heroic and those who fighting against their will were still ready to kill others rather than stand by their own principles. No man can be made to fight. No man fought in this war entirely against his will and, by God, as he would do unto others so let it be done unto him. If this war had appreciably diminished the proportion of the mass of men whose only religion is patriotism so servile that at the beck of their masters they give their lives in fawning gratitude to a country that had already robbed them of everything else, then in the name of everlasting Peace and for the greatest good of mankind the war had justified itself. There are those to whom the people of this land have so generously dispensed their partial favors that, if for the luxuries of life a man may be held to owe that life itself, it may be owe their lives to their country. But no man who toils and lives by the profit that his toil affords him owes anything to man or God. He is free. Let us now before another crisis arrives call upon our country for a declaration of the unpaid for favors that we have accepted of. Haply we may then balance the account at a cost to some of us of less than our lives and so order our lives for the future that no man or government may declare us in their debt.

It is late, Rockwell is asleep, the room is cold, it seems out of doors. There are no events of this day to record. It began gloriously fair and ended overcast but the hidden sun pouring a stream of golden light from behind our mountain onto the far off hills. In the mail that Olson brought us were a great package of warm woollen things for Rockwell and me from my mother, a sweater and a helmet cap for me from Auntie Jo, some stockings and a cap for Rockwell from his mother, a book of Kenai Peninsula from Carl, and coffee, chocolate and a box of sewing things, again from mother. It was like Christmas here! The porcupine after all proves rather an amusing pet. When this morning we set him free he chose to

70

return to his cage. So all day long he wandered not far off needing only to be headed toward it to return to its safety. So we'll have a try at training him.

"The war is over," cried Olson as he landed. By all that's holy in life may the world have found through its mad war at least some fragrance of the peace and freedom that we discovered growing like a flower, wild on the borders of the wilderness. . . .

Long into night I read the mail, count sweaters, caps, and woollen stockings, all that the mail has brought. It is late, Rockwell is asleep, the room is cold, it snows out-of-doors. . . . And now instead of bed I'll stir the fire and begin my work.

THURSDAY, NOVEMBER SEVENTH

A true winter's day with the snow deep on the ground and the profound and characteristic winter silence of the out-of-doors to be sensed even in this ever silent place. At earliest daylight began a heavy thunderstorm with lightning all about and a downpour of hail. It occurred intermittently throughout the morning. . . . I did the washing, using Olson's washboard and getting the clothes nearly white.

Olson is full of amusing gossip. To the curious in Seward who asked him why I chose to be in this Godforsaken spot he replied: "You damn fools, you don't understand an artist at all. Do you suppose Shakespeare wrote his plays with a silly crowd of men and women hanging around him? No, sir, an artist has to be left alone."

"Well, what does he paint?"

"That's his business. Sometimes I see he has a mountain there on a picture, and next time I see it's been changed to a lake or something else."

One can imagine Olson with his questioners. The thing he most wants, his ambition, one might say, is to make people sit up and take notice of Fox Island, his homestead. It is in fact one reason why he brought us here to live. Thanks to its amateur detective, Seward had rejoiced for a short time in rumors of a German spy on Fox Island. I told Olson that the authorities might still come and remove me. He flared up, "I'd like to see them try it! We could take to the mountains with guns, and more than one of them would never try the thing again." And then he went on to tell me how in Idaho he had tracked for days and weeks a notorious gang of outlaws and horse-thieves and at last run them to earth,—one of his most thrilling and, I believe, absolutely true stories of his adventures.

Meal Time

At this moment a steamer is blowing in the bay, navigating by the echo from the mountain faces. She is near to us now but hidden by the snowstorm.

Rockwell has begun to write the story of a long, waking dream of his. It's a sweet idea and reads most amusingly in his own queer spelling. Now, though it is already late, I must draw a while longer and then, after bathing in the bread pan, sit up in bed and read a chapter of the life of Blake. *That reading before I sleep is now my nightly practice and it is my one recreation and a real delight.*

Friday, November Eighth

It is so late that I half expect to see the dawn begin. I have been working on a drawing of Rockwell and his father—and it looks ever so fine.

Whew! just at this moment the wind has swept down upon our cabin and blown the roof in as far as it would with great creaking yield,—and then passed on sucking it out in its wake to such a spread that a board that lay across overhead like a collar-beam has fallen with a crash and clatter,—and Rockwell sleeps on! The wind does blow to-night, and it doesn't stop outside the walls of the cabin either. My lamp flutters annoyingly. But ah! the room is comfortable and warm.

This morning, it being at first wondrously fair, Rockwell and I set out for a boat ride. But what with the fussing of installing our motor and the launching of our cumbersome boat the wind was given time to rise and spoil the day for us. But we went out into the bay and played in the waves to see what the north wind could do. The chop was devilish, short and deep; the boat bridged from one crest to another with, it seemed, a clear tunnel underneath,—and then running up onto a wave mountain she would jump off its dizzy peak landing with a splash in the valley beyond and dousing us well with water. In a calmer spot I stopped the engine and sketched our island; after which we rowed home. The rest of the day we worked on the motor—first to find out why she wouldn't run, then, having found and fixed that, to put other parts in still better order, and then, by far the longest time and still to continue to-morrow, to mend what in the course of our fixing we had broken.

Saturday, November 9th. Fox Island

A gray day, a cold one, but how fine with the snow on the ground! Nothing accomplished but the engine mended and some wood cut. We have yet to

Day's End

eat dinner though it's about dark. Rockwell sports a pair of "Ladies boots"
that Olson had in keeping for some possible emergency.

Tuesday, November 12th. Fox Island

The pond is frozen hard and thick. Yes, today Rockwell skated and today
we both did. It was still and cold on the pond and wonderful for skating.
Rockwell does pretty well for a child beginner. He'll stick at it I believe
and if the skating lasts be himself a skater by the end of winter. If only
there were others of our friends here for the winter sports! I'm tempted to
build an ice boat. The lake is ideal for it.

Rockwell's in bed, asleep, dreaming of the little, wild nightingale that
sang of freedom to that poor, unhappy Chinese Emperor; while far from
here in streets and towns the tin nightingale of law-made liberty charms
the world. And it's now my reading time, my time for bread and jam and
a soft-cushioned back.

The days run by, true winter days, snow, cold, and wind,—what wind!
It is terrifying when from our mountain tops those fierce blasts sweep
upon us roaring as they come; flying twigs and ice beat on the roof, the
boards creak and groan under the wind's weight, the lamp flutters, moss
is driven in and falls upon my work-table, the canvas over our bed flaps,—
and then in a moment the wind is gone and the world is still again save
for the distant wash of the waves and the far off forest roar.

Olson is full of treats. His latest was in pleasant violation of the law.
From a bottle of pale liquid half filled with raisins he poured me a drink,
mixing it with an equal amount of ginger ale and a dash of sugar. It tasted
pretty good, quite thrilling in fact.

"What is it?" I asked.

"Pure alcohol," he said, smacking his lips.

Olson then launched forth on confidential advice, "from one trapper
to another," on how to trap men,—in my case rich patrons. He has my
need of them quite upon his mind.

Olson's eggs, by the way, taste good enough. (They gave him in Seward
twenty-four dozen bad eggs to bring out for the foxes.) We have eaten
a dozen. To-day I cracked seventeen to find six for dinner. Onion omelette
is the fashion to cook them in. Rockwell pronounces them delicious and—
well—so do I.

Hard, hard at work, little play, not too much sleep. The wind blows
ceaselessly. Rockwell is forever good,—industrious, kind, and happy. He

stopped the engine and sketched an island after which we rowed home. The rest of the day we worked on the motor – first to find why she wouldn't run, then, having found that, to put other parts in still better order, and then, by far the largest thing, and still to continue to-morrow, to mend what in the course of our firing we had broken. Thus – Olsen & I.

"Water Babies" is finished! that an event. When Kingsley isn't moralizing, his showing off, and nish his religious cant and his English snobbery he is, in spite of occasional sweet sentiment, quite unendurable. So to-night we read from Andersens fairy tales – forever lovely and true. And now my reading time is at hand, my time for bread and jam and a soft cushioned back.

76

reads now quite freely from any book. Drawing has become a natural and regular occupation for him, almost a recreation—for he can draw in both a serious and a humorous vein. At this moment he's waiting in bed for some music and another Andersen fairy tale.

WEDNESDAY, NOVEMBER 13TH. FOX ISLAND

It is a lovely moonlit night. How late it is again I do not know. I've worked hard the last three nights on an elaborate pen and ink chart of the island. It is now almost done, fortunately for my eyes. These are all days of such incessant work that unless I drag my hopes and fears over my pictures out for subject matter for this, Rockwell's book, there's little to fill the pages. However the days do vary slightly and every little thing that we do yields us so much pleasure that it is perhaps worth perpetuating to refresh some time the failing memory of the aged Rockwell, Jr. We do have fun. We fool hilariously, over the dish washing, racing in the morning at getting up time, at every moment that I'm not too busy or pre-occupied—for I do recollect mighty often that I'm not doing my full part here unless I become a nine year old child for my son's amusement just as he becomes a four legged creature at times for the astonished goats.

We skated to-day and Rockwell, wearing real shoes instead of the strange "ladies" boots that he usually sports, did quite wonderfully. Rockwell did his full duty and more in reading, writing and drawing pictures, amusing himself a lot over a pictorial history of a sea fight between himself in a ship of his own making, on the one hand, and Olson and myself on the other.—And now to put apricots to soak, a chapter—and one of the last—of the life of Blake, and sleep.

Another day has gone and a new morning is hours on its way. Out in the moonlit night strained, tired eyes open wide and are made clear again, cramped knees must dance in the crisp air, the curved spine bends backward as the upstretched arms describe that superb embracing gesture of the good-night yawn. November the thirteenth! how time sweeps by. And I look over the black water that we soon must cross again to Seward. The wind bursts around the cabin corner. I shiver and—go to bed.

V. WAITING

Thursday, November fourteenth.—We're ready to go to Seward the moment the weather moderates—which may be not for two weeks or two months. I've packed blankets and several days' food in a great knapsack so that if we're driven to land somewhere we'll not perish of hunger. And this trip while it may be carried out speedily may on the other hand strand us days without number in Seward and cost three or four times that many dollars.

The wind is still in the North, the days are wonderfully beautiful, and the nights no less. This very night Rockwell and I skated for the third time. Ah, but it was glorious on the lake, the moon high above us in a cloudless sky, the snow and ice on the mountain sides glistening and the spruces black. We skated together hand in hand like sweethearts; going far to one end of the lake in the teeth of the wind and returning before it like full-rigged ships. And Rockwell whose second skate to-day this was improves every minute.

I've cut Rockwell's hair, four months' growth. He has had the appearance of a boy of the Middle Ages with his hair cut to a line above his eyes. Now he's truly a handsome fellow—and such a man under the hardships of this cold place and rough life that I'm very proud of him.

SATURDAY, NOVEMBER SIXTEENTH

Still it blows, yesterday and to-day, cold, clear, and blue,—and the moon these nights stands straight above us and stays till dawn, setting far in the north. It is really cold. Olson is quite miserable and wonders how we can keep at our wood cutting and skating. But I think I shall never live *in* such cold again as in that first winter on Monhegan in my unfinished house when on cold days the water pails four feet from the stove froze over between the times I used them, and my beans at soak froze one night on the lighted stove. We love this weather here. While the cabin is drafty I pile on fuel remorselessly, and that's a real delight after having all my life had truly to count the pieces of coal and wood. The ice on the pond is six inches thick, part of it clear black that one can see the bottom through. This morning Rockwell changed to heavy underwear. He complains always of the heat, day and night.

The days go on about as usual varied only by an occasional weekly or monthly chore and success or failure in my painting. This morning with Olson's help I brought my boat up onto the land above the beach. The boat is an extremely heavily built eighteen-foot dory with a heavy keel; and yet the wind carried it four feet last night and, if it had not been secured, might have blown it down into the water where the waves would soon have wrecked it. This night I shall not read in bed; it's quite too far away from the stove.

SUNDAY, NOVEMBER SEVENTEENTH

We jumped from bed in a hurry this morning believing that the apparent stillness boded a calm day and a fit one for the Seward trip. But the sea beyond our cove was running swiftly and within two hours there was a gale of wind and some snow. Cold it was and dark. We'd hardly put the lamp out after breakfast, before we lighted it again for late dinner. Still in that short daylight I painted and Rockwell skated and painted, and we both cut a lot of wood. I've spent the evening writing, trying an article for "The Modern School." We turned my boat over and secured it to the ground with ropes just in time to escape the fall of snow to-night that lies deep on the ground. The moon is up and through the clouds there comes a general illumination like daylight.

MONDAY, NOVEMBER EIGHTEENTH

To-day a storm from the southeast. It blows like fury. Breakfast by lamplight, work until dark, then dinner—in the neighborhood of three o'clock or maybe four—more work, and a nap, for I felt exhausted. Rockwell goes to bed and is read to, I work a while longer, then a light supper for which Rockwell gets up again, then—the dishes washed and R. again in bed—a

I WANT TO BED ONE NIGHT, AND
DREAMED ABOWT NAIMALS. HWILE
FATHER SAT UP AND THIS IS MY

DREAM. I AND MY FATHER WANT HUNT—
ING IN THE WOODS. HWERE THER A—
RE WILDCATS, WILD PIGS, WOLVS, DEERS,
LIONS, BEARS, RABETS, PORKEAPINS, ELLOFONTS,
FOXS, AND TIGRS WE WERE WANDRING THRO
THE WOODS AND THR WOSANT A LEAV TWINGKL
OR A BOSH KRAKING WHAN OLLOSDON THREE
BOSHS KRAKEO. BOT WE DID NOT NO WHOT
IT WAS I RAN UP THE TREE WHILE
FATHER HID BEHINED A TREE HE
WOS GOWING TO SHOOT HIS GON BUT I
TOLD HIM NOT TO SHOOT HIS GON BE—
KOS I WONT TO KACH HIM. WHILE
I WAS SITING IN THE TREE. I
THAT HOW TO BE NICE TO HIM. I TOR
LEAVS OFF OF THE TREE. AND
I MADE A NIC SUIT OF LEAVS. I
TIDE THE LEAVS TO GETHER WITH STRING.

A BEAR

call on Olson for three quarters of an hour, leaving there at ten, to work, again till some wild hour. What a strangely arranged day! I'm determined to have a clock. But now it will be seen that no more time must be spent this night upon this diary. Amen.

TUESDAY, NOVEMBER NINETEENTH

A dreary, dreary, a weary day. But I've worked or somehow been ceaselessly busy and now I'm about ready for my nightcap of reading and bed. Four canvases stretched and primed stand to my credit and that alone is one day's work in effort and conquered repugnance. What a tedious work. My Christmas letters are written, nearly all of them. And as Christmas draws near it seems more and more impossible without home and the children. It will be a huge make-believe for one of our family here!

There's a big storm at sea from the look of the water and the sound of the wind. And the rain falls drearily and on the roof it rattles. From the tall trees the great drops fall like stones; they beat to pieces, little by little, the paper roof, and now when the rain is hardest we hear the drip, drip of the water on the floor. But we are comfortable—so what of it all.

I read "Big Claus and Little Claus" to Rockwell tonight. That's a great story and we roared over it. Rockwell doesn't like the stories about kings and queens, he says, "They're always marrying and that kind of stuff." Just the same Rockwell himself has his life and marriage pretty closely planned,—the journey from the East alone, the wife to be found at Seattle to save her carfare—and yet not put off as far as Alaska, for there they don't look nice enough,—and then life in Alaska to the end of his days. And I'm to be along if I'm not dead,—as I probably shall be, he says.

I have just finished the life of Blake and am now reading Blake's prose catalogue, etc., and a book of Indian essays of Coomaraswamy. The intense and illuminating fervor of Blake! I have just read this: "The human mind cannot go beyond the gift of God, the Holy Ghost. To suppose that Art can go beyond the finest specimens of Art that are now in the world is not knowing what Art is; it is being blind to the gifts of the Spirit." Here in the supreme simplicity of life amid these mountains the spirit laughs at man's concern with the form of Art, with new expression because the old is outworn! It is man's own poverty of vision yielding him nothing, so that to save himself he must trick out in new garb the old, old commonplaces, or exalt to be material for art the hitherto discarded trivialities of the mind.

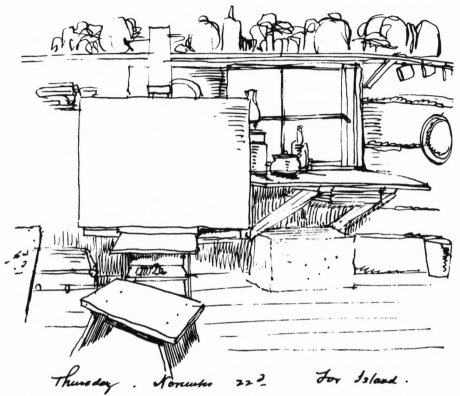

Thursday . November 22ᵈ.   Fox Island .

Yesterday and to-day are to be recorded.
The Porcupine (~~Walter after Walter Pach~~) is
dead ! And yesterday he endeared himself
so to us playing about in the house with
the utmost content . . The cause of his
death we cannot know unless it was our
kindness . Rockwell , with Olson's leather mitten
on did carry him about a good deal . Of
course they are creatures nocturnal and we
had planned to let him have his regular
hours for exercise and feeding , Rockwell

Wednesday, November Twentieth

To-morrow we hope to get off—although it still storms. There's a terrific sea running but even such a sea would trouble us less than the chop of the north wind. The wind above all else is to be feared here.

I painted little—it was so dark. Somehow on these short days it is difficult to accomplish much. Certain things have to be done by daylight: the chopping of wood, carrying of water from a hundred yards away, lamp filling, and some cooking. I made myself a lot of envelopes to-day and second-coated the canvases of yesterday's stretching. And now it is bedtime for to-morrow we rise early. Oh! the porcupine returned to-day and was discovered feeding calmly near the cabin. He showed no alarm at Rockwell's approach, and, when finally after some hours of undisturbed nibbling and napping Rockwell carried him home by his tail and set him down a little distance from his old cage, he ran straight there and interned himself.

Friday, November Twenty-second

Both yesterday and to-day are to be recorded. The porcupine is dead! And yesterday he endeared himself so to us, playing about in the house with the utmost content. The cause of his death we cannot know—unless it was our kindness. Rockwell with Olson's leather mittens on did carry him about a good deal. Of course they are creatures nocturnal and we had planned to let him have his regular hours for exercise and feeding, Rockwell delighting in the plan that he should stay with him in the woods at night, which I was certainly going to let him try. But it's over,—and Pet No. 2 has gone to his happy hunting grounds.

It storms, yesterday violently with such wind and rain as seemed incredible. The thin paper roof made the noise deafening so that I could not sleep; and the surf beat and the forest roared; it was a wild night. To-day is better though it pours every half hour. When, when shall we get to Seward! And here before me are displayed all the pretty Christmas presents I have made and that Rockwell has made. Here we sit, these dark short days, working together at the same table just like two professional craftsmen. On these days I cannot paint,—and Olson calls upon us more than he should. Still, we let him sit here in silence and he is wise enough to be quite content. Now it is late. The stove is out and I must go to bed. Two meals only to-day,—another is due me. Oh! I made myself a beautiful die for note paper yesterday and printed it on my envelopes to-day.

sit here in silence and he is nice
enough to be quite content. Now it
is late. The stove is out and I
must go to bed. Two meals only today,
another one is due me. — Oh — I
made myself a beautiful die for my note
paper yesterday and to-day printed it
on my envelopes with this press, shown
below, and oil paint for ink.
It worked pretty

Push Down.

well.

Friday, November 23ᵈ. Fox Island.
    It dawned calm with rain hanging
in the air. We hurried with our
breakfast in the hope that we should
get off; but within an nor at the
turn of the tide the North east wind
whipped down from the mountains and
the rain fell in torrents. And now
a late hour of the night it still rains
although the wind has fallen. We
felled a tree to-day and partly cut it
up. Although it was dismally dark all

85

Saturday, November Twenty-third

It dawned calm with rain hanging in the air. We hurried with our break-fast in the hope that we should get off; but within an hour at the turn of the tide the northwest wind whipped down from the mountains and the rain fell in torrents. And now at a late hour of the night it still rains although the wind has fallen. We felled a tree to-day and partly cut it up. Although it was dismally dark all the time I managed to paint a little. And I wrote much and drew in black and white. Rockwell has been industrious as usual, drawing at my side. He told me an amusing anecdote of little Kathleen that is worthy to go down here. When in play she wants to change her doll's name she sends for the pretend doctor, again herself, and he operates on the doll. Cutting a hole in her stomach he stuffs into it a little piece of paper on which he has written the new name. And so the name is changed.

Tried some cottonseed oil of Olson's to-day that was too bad. A year or two ago he was given a case of spoiled mayonnaise dressing for fox food. Olson saved the oil which had separated from the rest of it. I made dough for doughnuts while I heated the oil to fry ourselves that great treat. Then arose a pinching, rancid odor that almost made me ill but which Rock-well called delicious. However I baked the doughnuts. Still, the oil unheated seemed not bad.

Sunday, November Twenty-fourth

Olson declares this day to be Sunday and in honor of the day he gave me a cup of milk for junket. And in honor of the day, whatever it is, I worked so hard that now I'm tired out. The day began with snow and continued with it. It blustered and blew much as a day in March and the bay looked wild. And now to-night it is clear and starlight. Will the north wind begin to blow again to-morrow? The chances are that it will and Seward and the sending of my mail will be as far away as ever. I painted with some success for the snow makes the cabin lighter. Really my picture looks well. Eight canvases are far along so that I'm proud of them. We cut wood to-day of course; it would be great fun if only we'd more minutes of daylight to spare. Steamer must be due in Seward now. We've seen none for two weeks or longer.

The Cabin Window

Monday, November Twenty-fifth

It rages from the northeast! The bay is a wild expanse of breakers. They bear into our cove and thunder on the beach. A mad day and a wild night. And Seward is as far off as ever! It is now my hope that a steamer will go to Seward before me. Olson finds by his diary that none has been seen to go there for two weeks. I began two new pictures to-day trying for the first time to paint after dark. My lamp is so inadequate in this dark interior—it burns only a three-quarter inch wick—that I can work only in black and white. But I've laid in the whole picture in that way. Rockwell spends several hours a day out-of-doors exploring the woods, searching out porcupine trails and caves. It is weeks since I have stopped my work even for a walk. In this "out-of-doors life" I see little of out-of-doors. It's a blessing to me to have to saw wood every day.

I finished Coomaraswamy's "Indian Essays" to-day, an illuminating and inspiring book. Coomaraswamy defines mysticism as a belief in the unity of life. The creed of an artist concerns us only when we mean by it the tendency of his spirit. (How hard it is to speak of these intangible things and not use words loosely and without exact meaning.) I think whatever of the mystic is in a man is essentially inseparable from him; it is his by the grace of God. After all, the qualities by which all of us become known are those of which we are ourselves least conscious. The best of me is what is quite impulsive; and, looking at myself for a moment with a critic's eye, the forms that occur in my art, the gestures, the spirit of the whole of it is in fact nothing but an exact pictorial record of my unconscious living idealism.

Tuesday, November Twenty-sixth

After a terribly stormy and cold night the day was fair with the wind comfortably settled in the north as if he meant to stay there. Only at night has it been calm. To-night again is so and if I had not Rockwell on my hands to make me timid I'd go at night to Seward. Olson was a real Santa Claus to-day. First he gave us Schmier Käse, then a good salt salmon—two years old which he said we'd "better try"—and to-night a lot of butter churned by him from goat's milk. It looks like good butter and, with the added coloring matter, more palatable than the natural white butter of the goat. We felled two trees to-day—fairly small ones. We consume a vast amount of wood with our all-night fire. Well—to-morrow, let us say again, we'll be off to Seward.

"Go to Bed"

Wednesday, November Twenty-seventh

To-day, if we had known how the weather would turn, we should have started. It was lovely, cold but fair with the wind in the southwest. It had in the morning all appearances of a heavy blow and we failed to get in shape to take advantage of its calming as the afternoon advanced. At any rate I have a little picture of it with the soft haze of the day and the loose clouds. I painted besides on the large canvas of Superman begun a few days ago. Olson lent me his "grub-box" to use, a wooden box of small grocery size with a cover fastened with a strap and buckle. Such a box is part of the outfit of every man on the Yukon. My emergency grub is now in it, my letters, Christmas presents, and all that's bound for Seward. Rockwell took Squirlie out for an airing to-day, wrapping him with tender care in a sweater. They went for a long way into the woods like good companions. Then Rockwell drew a portrait of his muffled pet which is destined for Clara's Christmas.

Thursday, November Twenty-eighth

This continual waiting is getting upon my nerves. Most of to-day I spent tinkering with the engine. It goes now—in a water barrel. The trouble with the best of these little motors is that the moment they get wet they stop, and they are attached at such an exposed place, on the stern, that they will get wet if there's much of a sea. Then you're in a bad fix for it's impossible to make any headway rowing with the engine—or rather the propeller—dragging. Most of the engines are hung right on the stern and can be readily detached and drawn into the boat. But mine fits into a sort of pocket built in the stern and is difficult even on land to lift out. It weighs decidedly over a hundred pounds. So I don't relish getting caught with such an equipment. I must have mentioned, by the way, that the engine was "thrown in" with the boat as of no value.

So there's the day gone. To-night we go to bed early and if it is calm just before daylight in the morning we shall start at once.

Friday, November Twenty-ninth

Last night a terrific storm from the east. A few blasts struck the house with such force that it seemed our thin roof could not stand it. Of course it is really quite strong enough but the noise of those sudden squalls bearing along snow and ice from the tree tops is simply appalling. In the morning it became milder but continued to rain and snow and for most of the

Driftwood

day to blow heavily from the eastward. In the afternoon to my despair a steamer entered for Seward; she'll doubtless leave at daylight. There goes one of my chances to get my Christmas mail off.

I painted splendidly to-day and am in the seventh heaven over it,— which takes away some of my gloom at never reaching Seward. A long call from Olson to-night. He sits here patiently and silently while I draw. It snows steadily. What will to-morrow bring?

Francis Galton, the inquirer into human faculty, would have been charmed at Rockwell's casual mention of the colors of proper names. They do apparently assume definite colors that seem to him appropriate and characteristic beyond question. Clara, too, sees names as colors. Father is blue, Mother is a darker blue. The breadth of vowel sound apparently, judging from this and other examples he gave me, lowers the tone of color. Kathleen is a light yellow, very light. Now for a bite to eat, for I've had but two meals—and then to bed.

VI. EXCURSION

Thursday, December fifth.—November thirtieth we arose before daylight. It was a mild, still morning and the melting snow dripped from the trees. Without breakfast we set about at once to carry our things over to the boat. Olson was aroused and turned out to help. There's always much to be carried on a trip to Seward; gasoline, oil, tools, my pack bag—containing clothes, heavy blankets, and spare boots,—and the grub box Olson had given me packed with mail, books, grub, and the flute. The engine was in good order and started promptly. So away we went out over the bay just as the day brightened.

It was calm and beautiful. The sun from below the horizon shot shafts of light up into the clouds, gray became pink, and pink grew into gold until at last after an hour or more the sun's rays lighted up the mountain peaks, and we knew that he had risen. It continued calm and mild all the way, but nevertheless I caught myself singing "Erlkönig," such is my anxiety at carrying Rockwell with me. Rockwell enjoyed the trip wrapped up in a sheepskin coat of Olson's. We stopped at a fishing camp for a moment's chat from the water. The man living there had just caught a good-sized wolverine. We declined breakfast and hurried on.

In Seward we stored our things in Olson's cabin, a little place about eight feet square, and started for the hotel. One of our friends met us with a shout. "Well, you've had good sense to stay away so long."

93

Influenza, I then learned, had raged in Seward, there having been over 350 cases; and smallpox had made a start. But the deaths had been few and it was now well in hand. However, I shunned the hotel. A little cottage was generously put at our disposal and we were soon comfortably settled there with our mail from home spread before us. I left everything of mine at the hotel untouched and we continued to wear our old clothes throughout the stay. At midnight I went with Otto Boehm to pull the dory up above the tide and overturn her, and then continued letter writing until three-thirty A. M.

December first and every day of our stay at Seward was calm and fair. We kept house in our cottage, I continually busy writing and doing up Christmas presents, for a steamer had entered on the thirtieth and was due to leave Sunday night, the first. *Rockwell found the boys of Seward more friendly and spent the day going about out of doors. That night I played and sang at the postmaster's house and had a fine time.* The people of Seward are friendly without being the slightest bit inquisitive, and they are extremely broad-minded for all that their country is remote from the greater world. I don't believe that provincialism is an inevitable evil of far-off communities. The Alaskan is alert, enterprising, adventurous. Men stand on their own feet, and why not? The confusing intricacy of modern society is here lacking. The men's own hands take the pure gold from the rocks; no one is another's master. It's great land—the best by far I have ever known.

What a telltale of reaction from our lonely island life is this roseate vision of the little city of the far northwest! We came in time to see Seward quite differently and, with confidence in Alaska, to believe it to be in no way a typical and true Alaskan town. The "New York of the Pacific," as it is gloriously acclaimed in the literature of its Chamber of Commerce, numbers its citizens perhaps at half a thousand—the tenacious remnant of the many more who years ago trusted our government to fulfill its promises to really build and operate a railroad into the interior. One's indignation fires at the recital of the men of Seward's wrongs,—until you recollect that Seward was built for speculation, not for industry, and that by the chance turn of the wheel many have merely reaped loss instead of profit. There are no resources at that spot to be developed and there is consequently no industry.

Seward is planned for growth and equipped for commerce. Wide avenues and numbered blocks adorn the town-site maps where to the

The Whittler

naked eye the land's a wilderness of stumps and briars. The center of the built-up portion of the town, one street of two blocks' length, is modern with electric lights and concrete pavements. The stores are wonderfully good; there are two banks and several small hotels, a baker from Ward's bakery in New York and a French barber from the Hotel Buckingham. There's a good grammar school, a hospital, and churches of all sorts. There is no public library; apparently one isn't badly missed. Seward's a tradesmen's town and tradesmen's views prevail,—narrow reactionary thought on modern issues and a trembling concern at the menace of organized labor. A strike of the three newsboys of the Seward paper plunged the poor fool its printer into frantic fear of an I. W. W. plot. But even Seward smiled at the little man's terror. The worst of Seward is itself; the best is the strong men that by chance are there or that pass through from the great Alaska.

December second was a day for shopping. I bought all manner of Christmas things, things for the tree, things to eat, little presents for Olson, but nothing for Rockwell. He and I must do without presents this Christmas. Then more letters were written. A wood block that I had cut proved, on my seeing a proof of it, to be absolutely worthless. *That night I called on Thwaites—the photographer of Seward who makes all the post card views. He's a most intelligent and interesting man of a most varied experience. So the evening passed well. Rockwell went that evening to Brownell's house where the great fire place is and a fine phonograph. They like Rockwell a lot. He left early and went home to bed alone.*

December third I had still so much mail and business to attend to that I stayed over another day. Set a door frame for Brownell and spent that evening at his house. The postmaster came too, fine fellow, and we'd a great evening taking turns singing songs—and the P. M. did mighty well with "School-master Mishter O'Toole." The day I'd spent writing and gossiping about town. *Brosius and Noon, the contractors of Seward, are the best of fellows. Old Noon a pioneer of the country who is now "well fixed" and made his money himself. Brosius, a shrewd all round mechanic and smart man. He's making half a dozen dog sleds to carry mail inland. They're to cost $125.00 each and are worth it. Beautiful things, light, strong and graceful.*

I heard then a story about Olson that's worth while. He was once telling a crowd of men about the reindeer to the northward. Among his listeners was a Jew who was annoyed with his "hectoring." At last this joker asked:

"Olson, if you bred a reindeer to a Swede what would you get?" "You'd get a Jew," replied Olson. The Jew, who still lives in Seward, has not bothered Olson since. The old man has a rare reputation for his honesty and truth and all round sterling qualities. *Met Dr. Sloane of Seward that evening. He's a Scotchman with a string of professional letters to his name. At any rate most cordial and invites me to dinner on my next visit there. The truth is McCormack of the S.P.R.R. has certainly been boosting me as I learned from several men. I received in the mail a letter from the Manager of the Copper River Railroad offering me a free trip over their lines and back. I've accepted it for next spring. McCormack did that.*

It's truly a satisfaction to be in a country where men are alert enough to take no offense at alertness, where enterprise is so common a virtue that it arouses no suspicion, and where it is the rule to mind your own business.

December fourth we set about to leave for Fox Island. It took two hours to wind up our final business in town and embark. Brownell helped with the boat. Of course the engine balked for fifteen minutes and then (not "of course") went beautifully. After traveling a quarter of a mile I learned that Rockwell had left our clock standing in the snow by Olson's cabin. So for that we went back. Brownell saw us and brought it. *But after all a box of Christmas fruit remained in Seward in that cabin. It was a present to us from Hawkins.*

The trip was swift and smooth. At Caine's Head it began to snow, obscuring Fox Island, but I knew the course. In mid-channel the engine stopped. After ten minutes' tinkering it resumed going and went beautifully till we rounded the head of our cove. Then it sputtered and I had continually to crank it. However, it carried us to thirty or forty feet of the shore when it breathed its last, thanks to the snow that had by now thoroughly wet the engine and ourselves. We unloaded and with great labor hauled up the dory and turned her over. That night I was exhausted and went straight to bed, leaving Rockwell at his drawing. So now we're on Fox Island again.

VII. HOME

Thursday, December fifth (Continued).—Mild, rainy, snowy, sleepy—this first day back at home.

I've done little work and dared look at but one picture—that of Superman—and it appears truly magnificent. The sky of it is luminous as with northern lights, and the figure lives. After all it is Life which man sees and which he tries to hold and in his Art to recreate. To that end he bends every resource straining at what limits him. If he could only be free, free to rise beyond the limits of expression into being! at his prophetic vision of man's destiny assuming himself the lineaments of it, in stature grown gigantic, rearing upwards beyond the narrow clouds of earth into the unmeasured space of night, his countenance glowing, his arms outstretched in an embrace of wider worlds! This is the spirit and the gesture of Superman.—So I'm not unhappy. Now work begins again. For weeks there'll be no mail in Seward and for more weeks none here.

FRIDAY, DECEMBER SIXTH

I'm reading a little book on Dürer. What a splendid civilization that was in the Middle Ages, with all its faults. To men with my interests can anything be more conclusive proof of the superiority of that age to this than the position of the artist and the scholar in the community? Let me quote from Dürer's diary. (Antwerp, a banquet at the burgomaster's hall.)

"All their service was of silver, and they had other splendid ornaments and very costly meats. All their wives were there also. And as I was being led to the table the company stood on both sides as if they were leading some great lord. And there were among them men of very high position, who all treated me with respectful bows, and promised to do everything in their power agreeable to me that they knew of. And as I was sitting there in such grandeur, Adrian Horebouts, the syndic of Antwerp, came with two servants and presented me with four cans of wine in the name of the Town Councillors of Antwerp, and they bid him say that they wish thereby to show their respect for me and assure me of their good will. Wherefore I returned my humble thanks—etc. After that came Master Peeter, the town carpenter, and presented me with two cans of wine, with the offer of his willing services. So when we had spent a long and merry time together till late at night, they accompanied us home with lanterns in great honor."

Oh land of porcelain bath-tubs! A man has only to leave all that by which we to-day estimate culture to realize that all of his own civilization goes with him right to the back woods, and lives there with him refined and undiminished by the hardships there.

Civilization is not measured by the poverty or the wealth of the few or of the millions, nor by monarchy, republicanism, or even Freedom, nor by whether we work with hands or levers,—but by the final fruit of all of these, that imperishable record of the human spirit, Art. The obituary of to-day in America has surely now been written in the poor workshop of some struggling, unknown man. That is all that the future will know of us.

All records for winds are broken by what rages tonight. From the northwest it piles into our cove. The windows are coated with salt, and tons of flying water sail in clouds out of the bay hiding the mountains from the base to half their height. Our rafters bend beneath the blast; ice— from we know not where—falls upon us with a thundering noise. The canvases suspended aloft sway and flap, and from end to end of the cabin the breeze roves at will. It's so ridiculously bad and noisy and cold that Rockwell and I just laugh. But the wood is plentiful for we cut some more to-day.

Last night at bedtime the wind had risen. At some midnight hour the stove went out for I awoke at two and found the cold about us and the wind hard at it. So with a generous use of kerosene the fire was made to

"Get Up!"

burn again and I returned to a good night's rest. Somehow one doesn't mind short exposures to the cold. Many a day I have stood naked out in the wind and then become at once glowing warm again in the hot cabin. Baked bread to-day and it turned out very well. Painted, shivered, wrote, and to-night shall try to design a picture of the "Weird of the Gods." But at this moment our supper is ready and two hungry, cold mortals cannot be kept from their corn mush.

SATURDAY, DECEMBER SEVENTH

Late! Now that we have a clock—I stole one in Seward—we live by system, our hours are regular. The clock I set by the tide, marking the rise of the water in the new-fallen snow. We rise at 7:30. It is then not yet sunrise but fairly light. Breakfast is soon cooked and eaten. To start the blood going hard for a good day's work we spring out-of-doors and chop and split and saw in the glorious, icy northwind. Then painting begins. I have scared Olson away—poor soul—but I make it up by calling on him just at dark when my painting hours are over.

Now it's eleven at night and I've still my bit to read. Whew, but it's cold to-night and the wind is rising to a gale. And last night!—what a bitter one. I got up four times to feed the ravenous fire. And even so the water pails froze. We cannot afford to let it freeze much in the cabin for our stores are all exposed. What if the Christmas cider should freeze and burst! I painted out of doors to-day—in sneakers! and stood it just about as long as one would imagine. To love the cold is a sign of youth—and we do love it, the Awakener.

SUNDAY, DECEMBER EIGHTH

Log cabins stuffed with moss should be wonderful in the tropics. I'm about frozen. On this work table I must weight my papers down to keep them from flying about the room. And the wind is icy; it is bitterly, bitterly cold. Olson says we need expect no colder weather than this all winter. Of course we don't really mind it. The stove is red hot and we may go as close to it as we please, and the bed is warm—except towards morning. At night I move my jugs of yeast and cider toward the stove, fill the "air-tight" to the top, pile blankets and wrappers upon the bed, and sleep happily.

The gale still rages, fortunately not with its utmost fury. This morning Rockwell and I hurried through our chores and then climbed to the low ridge of the island. The snow in the woods is crusted and bore us up well so that we traveled with ease and soon reached the crest. Ah, there it was glorious; such blue and gold and rose! We looked down upon the spit and saw the sea piling upon it; we looked seaward and saw the snow blown from the land, the spray and the mist rising in clouds toward the sun,—and the sun, the beautiful sun shone on us. We took a number of pictures and then with numbed fingers and toes raced down the slope playing man-pursued-by-a-bear. Rockwell was wonderful to look at with cheeks so red and clear. He loved our little excursion.

And for the rest of the day we've worked. I stretched and coated three large canvases, hateful job! painted, sawed wood, felled a tree—which the wind carried over onto another so that there it hangs neither up nor down, —and that's about all. It's again eleven and time for bed. The night is beautiful even if it is terrible; and the young moon is near setting.

Monday, December Ninth

It blows worse than ever, and it is colder. All day the blue sky has been hidden in clouds of vapor and flying spray. The bay seethes and smokes and huge breakers race across it. It is truly bitter weather. Olson to-night ventured the prophecy that this was about the culmination of winter—but I know Olson by now. I cut another tree this morning to release the one of yesterday and both fell with a magnificent crash. Then we went to work with the cross-cut saw and stocked our day's wood.

Olson called this afternoon and related his recollection of the early days of Nome.

"A certain man," he began, "deserted from a whaler that stopped for water on the north coast of Alaska. He'd been shanghaied in San Francisco and was a tailor by trade. He made his way down the coast with the occasional help of the esquimaux. At last he came to Nome. The men were gone from the native village but a woman took him in. She was named English Mary. Now she had heard of the gold finds on the Yukon and she asked the man if he was a miner. He answered, 'Yes.' 'You come with me,' she said, and led him to a certain creek and showed him the shining nuggets lying thick upon the bottom. But the tailor really knew nothing about gold and let it lie. He continued down the coast and was at last carried to St. Michael. There he met a missionary and a young fellow who had come to Alaska with a party of prospectors. With those two he returned in a boat to Nome. You'll hear different stories, to be

Man

sure, of how they got there but this is the right one, for I've seen the boat they came in lying there off the beach. Well, they came and saw the gold but none of them could say for certain what it was. So one of them went off to get a man from the party of prospectors with whom the young fellow had come to Alaska. At last they got him there and he proved that it was sure enough gold. They staked their claims and began to work them. But word of gold travels fast and already others began to come. The miner of that first party drew up mining laws for the country and these were enforced. I was up on the Yukon when I heard of the first find at Nome. I went down and arrived there in the fall, a little more than a year after the strike. By that time there was quite a number there.

"Some man had drawn up a plan of a town and was selling lots. I bought one on the northwest corner of the block. It was on the tundra. (Tundra is vegetation covered ice, soggy to a foot's depth.) There was a tent on my lot and some wood, so I bought those too. But shortly after when I came home one day from prospecting I found that both the tent and the wood had been stolen. I bought lumber for the frame of a new tent. It cost me thirty dollars; that is, fifty cents a foot. By that time all kinds of people were pouring into Nome. They were taking out gold on the creek, those that had claims, at the rate of $5000 in a couple of hours. It was so heavy in the sand you couldn't handle a pan-full.

"Someone cut into my tent and cleaned me out—but I had nothing much besides a jack-knife. I borrowed ten dollars and went to work at a dollar an hour. A couple of rascals had come there, a judge and a lawyer; and they began to get busy swindling everybody out of their titles to claims. It was said openly that if you saw anyone's claim 'jump it', and the lawyers would make more money for you than you could get out in gold. There was no use in a man without money trying to hold a claim. And the crowd that was there! Gamblers, sharps, actors,—men and women of every kind—and they did act so foolish!—all out of their heads over the gold. The brothels were running wide open and robberies occurred in the town by daylight. Every man slept with his gun beside him and if he shot it was to kill. The robbers chloroformed men as they slept in their tents. There were thousands of people then and you could look out on the beach and see them swarming like flies. Everything was overturned for gold,—the entire beach for ten miles both ways from Nome was shoveled off into the sea. They dug under the Indian village till the houses fell in, and even under the graveyard."

And so Olson's story continues. A story of his life would really be—as an old pioneer in Seward told me—a history of Alaska. Because Olson has never succeeded he has been everywhere and tried everything. I have not done him justice in my abridgment of his Nome story. His recollections are so intimate. He remembers the words spoken in every situation and never, no matter how much an adventure centers in himself, does he depart in what he tells of himself from his character as I know him.

I would not have devoted all of the time I have to this day's entry if I had not a good day's work to my credit including the conception of a new picture so vivid that the doing of it will be mere copying. It is the "North Wind." Surely after the past four days I may tell with authority of that wild Prince from the North.

Wednesday, December Eleventh

Yesterday was too gloomy a day for me to risk a page in this journal. As to weather it was another fierce one, cold and windy. As to work accomplished—nothing. Olson in his cabin, on such a day, is a treat to see. I open the door and enter. There he sits near the stove, a black astrakhan cap on his head and the two female goats in full possession of the cabin. Nanny the milch goat is a most affectionate creature. She lays her head on Olson's lap and as he scratches her head her eyes close in blissful content.

"See her pretty little face," says Olson, "and her lovely lips." He's certainly the kindest creature to animals—and to human ones too we have good reason to know.

To-day it is milder. The vapor is thick on the bay but it lies low upon the water and the magnificent mountains sparkle in the sunlight.

Work has gone better for me and it has been a day not without accomplishment. I baked bread—beautiful bread, cut wood, helped Olson a bit, and had a glorious rough-house with my son. He's a great fighter. I train him for the fights he's bound to have some day by letting him attack me with all his strength; and that has come to be not a little thing.

Friday, December Thirteenth

In the midst of letter writing I stop to note down a dramatic cloud effect. That's the way the day's work goes. If I'm out-of-doors busy with the saw or axe I jump at once to my paints when an idea comes. It's a fine life and more and more I realize that for me at least such isolation—not from my friends but from the unfriendly world—is the only right life for me.

106

Woman

My energy is too unrestrained to have offered to it the bait for fight and play that the city holds out, without its being spent in absolutely profitless and trivial enterprises. And here what a haven of peace! Almost the last touch is added to its perfection by the sweet nature of the old man Olson. I have never known such a man. I'm no admirer of the "picturesqueness" of rustic character. Seen close to it's generally damnably stupid and coarse. I have seen the working class from near at hand and without illusion. But Olson! he has such tact and understanding, such kindness and courtesy as put him outside of all classes, where true men belong.

To-night it looked like the picture I have drawn. These are beautiful days. Yesterday it was as calm in our little cove as one would look for on a summer's day. The day was blue and mild, a day for work. I made of my "North Wind" the most beautiful picture that ever was. I stood it facing outwards in the doorway and from far off it still showed as vivid, more vivid, and brilliant than nature itself. It's the first time I've taken my pictures into the broad light. There's where they should be seen.

Last night was calm until four o'clock in the morning. Then the wind again struck in and the trees roared and the roof creaked and groaned. To-day it was calmer. We began by felling a tall spruce more than two feet in diameter. It lies now near the cabin a great screen of evergreen. Its wood should last us many weeks. I painted out-of-doors on two pictures. That's bitterly cold work—to crouch down in the snow; through bent knees the blood goes slowly, feet are numbed, fingers stiffen. But then the warm cabin is near....

This minute I've returned from splitting wood out in the moonlight. On days when painting goes with spirit the chores are left undone.

If only it were possible to put down faithfully all of Olson's stories! Last night he told of his return to San Francisco from the Yukon thirty years ago, how the little band of weather-beaten, crippled miners appeared on their return to civilization. Olson was on crutches from scurvy, his beard and hair were of a year's growth; all were in their working clothes, all bearded, brown, free spirited. And their wealth they carried on them in bags, gold, some to $7000 worth. As Olson tells it you yourself live in that day. You hear the German landlady of the "Chicago Hotel" in San Francisco, a motherly woman who put all the grub on the table at once so you could help yourself, say, "You boys have some of you been in Alaska for years and I know about how you've lived. Now that you're back you must have a hankering for some things. Tell me whatever you want and

Foreboding

I'll get it for you." And up spoke one big fellow, "I remember how my mother used to have cabbage. I want you to get me one big head and cook it and let me have it all to myself!"

That night they went to the music halls in their miners' clothes all as they were, and drank gallons of beer; and from the boxes and the balconies the girls all clamored to be asked to join them—who were such free spenders. Two days later they were paid in coin for their gold—by the mint—and all went to the tailors and got them fine suits of clothes. . . . And so it continues. And he told of Custer's massacre. And, to-night of the sagacity of horses in leading a trapper back to the traps he'd set and maybe lost. When a horse swims with you across a stream guide him with your hand on his neck, but pull not ever so little on the line or he'll rear backwards in the water and likely drown himself and you.

Saturday, December Fourteenth

A pretty useless day. No work accomplished but the daily chores. What is there to say of such a day? Olson brought over his letter to Kathleen to-night and read it to us. It's just like him to be really himself even at letter writing. The letter is full of nice humor. "She'll think what kind of an old fool is that," he said, "but what do I care. I'll just say what ever I feel like saying." And he always does. In a mild way he lives Blake's proverb, "Always speak the truth and base men will avoid you." Some people have found Olson very rough and ill-mannered.

Made bread to-night and stamped about seventy-five envelopes with my device. To-night it is mild and overcast. A light snow has begun to fall. So far this winter the fall of snow has been extremely light. It should bank up almost to the cabin's eaves. . . . My bed awaits me. Good-night.

Sunday, December Fifteenth

This is another day that is hardly worth recording, one that would not be missed from a life.

It's time something were again said about young Rockwell who is the real, live, crowning beauty of the community. Weeks have passed since I last recorded his fresh delight in everything here. It is the same to-day. For hours he plays alone out-of-doors. Now he's an animal crawling on all fours along the trunk of a tree that I have felled, going out upon its horizontal branches as the porcupines do, hiding himself in the foliage and growling fiercely—hours long it seems—while the foolish goats flee

"And the people went there . . . and forgot themselves."

in terror and the foxes race wildly up and down the extent of their corral. Again he's a browsing creature eating the spruce needles with decided relish,—doing it so seriously. Truly he lives the part he plays when it is one of his beloved wild creatures. Then he tears up and down the beach mounted like a four-year-old kid on a stick horse, yelling as loud as he can, going to the water's edge, and racing the swell as it mounts the slope. And presently I capture him for his end of the saw. At that he no longer knows fatigue,—he's as good as a man. He really never tires and the work goes on with a fine, jolly good-will that makes of the hardest chore one of the day's pleasures. Rockwell is lonely at times; but if he tells me he'd like somebody to play with he's sure to add in the same breath, "Ah well, never mind."

I don't know how such a haphazard education if continued would fit him for participation in the "practical" affairs of life. But I am convinced that if all the little beauties of spirit that can now be seen budding could be allowed free, clean growth, quite away from the brutal hand of mass influences, we'd have nothing less than the full and perfect flowering of a human soul;—and in our reaching toward supermanhood none can do more.

Here, as an example, is an achievement of his imagination that it is hard to picture as surviving long in the atmosphere of a large school. Rockwell for two or three years has called himself the "mother of all things." It is not a figure of speech with him but an attitude towards life. If it were the creed of a great poet—and it could be—the discerning critic might discover it to be of the profoundest significance in modern thought. In little Rockwell it is of one piece with his whole spirit which expresses itself in his love for all animals, the fiercest to the mildest, and for all growing things. The least manifestation of that which is thought to be typical cruelty of boys outrages his whole nature.

I am far from believing Rockwell to be a unique example of childhood. I think that while cruelty appears uppermost where boys herd together, the love of animals is no less characteristic of many sensitive children. But of this I am certain,—that nothing will make a child more ridiculous in the eyes of the mob child than this most perfect and most beautiful attitude of some children toward life. In considering the education of a child and weighing what is to be gained or lost by one system or another I am inclined to think that no gain can outweigh the loss to a child of its loving, non-predatory impulses.

Monday, December 16th. Fox Island

I bear no resemblance to G. B., I swear it. I have shaved my head and polished it with oil and now, if ever, the structural similarity will be most evident. People have lied. Only when we come to be looked straight down upon from windows—marching perhaps as celebrities in parades—when only the shining fleshy surface of our domes shall be visible—and the tips of our noses—only then shall I admit the chance of real mistaken identity between us. Well—let it be recorded that on shaving my head at the age of thirty-six the dome was discovered to have a texture like the bulging surface of a hair-cloth sofa—smooth and glossy with occasional sharp prickles. Or maybe it's more like the cylinder of the old fashioned tinkling music boxes. That's it! and to change the tune I rub on kerosene and Castor Oil. I think that Olson's clippers, manipulated entirely by myself, and my razor have occupied me most of the day. It's all I can remember— but that the gently falling rain reminds me that the whole day has been mild, overcast and calm.

Tuesday, December Seventeenth

Once a miner died and presently found his way to the gates of heaven.

"What do you want?" said St. Peter.

"To come in, of course."

"What sort of man are you?"

"I'm a miner."

"Well," said Peter, "we've never had anyone of that kind here before, so I suppose you might as well come in."

But the miner once within the gates fell to tearing up the golden streets of heaven, digging ditches and tunnels all over the place and making a frightful mess of it all. At last a second miner presented himself at the gates.

"Not on your life," said St. Peter. "We have one miner here and we only wish we knew some way to get rid of him. He's tearing up the whole place."

"Only let me in," said the second miner, "and I'll promise to get rid of that fellow for you." So St. Peter admitted him.

This second miner easily found the other who was hard at work and amid a shower of flying earth. Going up to him he cried in an undertone: "Partner! They've struck gold in Hell!"

The miner dropped his work and sprang toward the gates. "Peter, Peter, open, open! Let me out of Heaven, I'm off to Hell!"

113

Lone Man

What a book of yarns and jokes this is becoming! Today work went a little better—and the weather a little worse. It pours. For the end of December it is wonderfully mild; but then I expect little really cold weather here. To-night it is full moon. The tide is at its highest for the year and the southeast wind piles the water up till it reaches and over-flows the land. Olson expects it to touch his house to-night if the wind continues. Tree trunks, uprooted somewhere from the soil, monstrous and grotesque, grind along our beach; the water is full of driftwood and wreckage.

Wednesday, December Eighteenth

There's a little bucket of dough that stands forever on the shelf behind the stove. Sour dough is made with yeast, flour, and water to the con-sistency of a bread sponge and then allowed to stand indefinitely. For all that you take out you add more flour and water to what's left in the bucket and that shortly is as fit for use as the original mixture. Alaskans use it extensively as the basis for bread and hot cakes. You add but a pinch of soda and a little water to the proper consistency and it's all ready for use. The old time Alaskans rejoice in the honorable title of "Sour Doughs."

Olson's cabin in Seward stands comfortably on a little lot in a quite thickly settled part of the town. I wondered at his affluence in possessing a house and lot. Here is its history as he told it to me to-night. When Olson first came to Seward he built—or he bought already built—a little cabin standing on a part of the beach now occupied by the railroad yard. In course of time he went to Valdez for a winter's work. Returning, he found no cabin. It was gone from that spot and he has not found it since. But corporations and governments are nothing to Olson when he feels himself injured. He went to one official and said, "See here! Winter's at hand and I have no house, what are you going to do about it?" Well, they would see what could be done, and in time referred him to a higher authority. "I want a cabin," Olson said to this one. "If you don't give me the lumber to build one with I'll have to steal it from you. I have no money and no cabin. Winter is here and I'm certainly going to live in a cabin this winter." So they gave him an old shed to tear down and use but told him not to build on the beach. The town of Seward was laid off in lots. By the stakes Olson could tell a lot from a street, and fair and square on a lot, somebody's lot, he put his cabin. The owner of the land was tolerant and let it stay there a few years; but one day he ordered Olson's house

Wednesday. December 18th. Fox Island.

Sour Dough Bucket.

Here a little bucket that stands on the shelf behind the stove. Sour Dough is made with yeast, flour and water of the consistency of a bread sponge and then allowed to stand indefinitely or for ever. For all that you take out you add more flour and water to what's left in the bucket and that shortly is as fit for use as the original mixture. Alaskans use it extensively as the basis for bread and hot cakes. You add but a pinch of soda and with thinness of flour or water to the proper consistency its all ready for use. The old time Alaskans are called "Sour Doughs".

116

Olsen's cabin in Seward stands completely on a little lot in a quite thickly settled part of the town. I wondered at his affluence in possessing a

Porridge Bowl.

Plate

Cup - holding 1 Pt. Robins egg Blue.

house and lot. Here is its history as he told it to me to-night. When Olsen first came to Seward he built — no he bought already built — a little cabin standing on a part of the track now occupied by the railway yard. In course of time he went to Valdez for a winter's work. Returning, he found no cabin. It was gone from that spot and he has not found it since. But corporations and governments are nothing to Olsen when he feels himself injured. He went to one official and said "See here! Winter's at hand and I have no house what are you going to do about it?" Well — they would see what could be done, and in time referred him to a higher authority. "I want a cabin" Olsen

taken off. So Olson carried it somehow out into the middle of the street where it fitted in nicely among the tree stumps. Well and good for a little time till in the summer before last the town of Seward improved that street and sent a man and team to remove the stumps. "If you're paid to remove the stumps you may as well move my house for me," said Olson. Where to?" asked the man. "You can suit yourself," said Olson. So the cabin was again planted on a "desirable" lot of somebody's,—and there it stands to-day, neat and trim, with a little wooden walk connecting its doorway with the plank sidewalk of the street. Alaska is, to be sure, a great free country!

To-day has been wonderfully mild and comfortable. From time to time the rain has fallen gently. Over the water the clouds have dropped, hiding the mountain peaks. The sea has been glassy save for the long swell—and this more to be heard upon the beach than seen. Rockwell and I at dusk walked the shore out to the point between the coves. We saw the glowing sky where the sun had set, the mountainous islands to the southward, and our own cove and its mountain ramparts—beautiful in the black and white of the spruces and the snow. If I but had my prepared canvas I'd make large studies of the many views from this point.

Rockwell at dinner begged me repeatedly to have part of his junket besides my own. I wondered at it for although he is always considerate and polite this was almost too much. And in other ways I noticed his alacrity to be obliging. Later in the day he told me, after much embarrassment, that he had made up his mind to be nicer about everything and to do more for me,—and yet I had previously found no fault with him; how could I! So ends a day;—and again I think that in this country I would gladly live for years.

Rockwell at dinner to-day begged me repeatedly to
have part of his junket besides his own.
I understand at it for although he is always
considerate and polite this was almost too much.
And in other ways I noticed his alacrity to
be obliging. Later in the day he told me,
after much embarrassment, that he had made
up his mind to be nicer about everything and
to do more for me. -- and I had previously
found no fault with him — How could I ?
So here ends a day — and again I think
that in this country I would gladly live for
years .

VIII. CHRISTMAS

Thursday, December nineteenth.—This day is never to be forgotten, so beautiful, so calm, so still with the earth and every branch and tree muffled in deep, feathery, new-fallen snow. And all day the softest clouds have drifted lazily over the heaven shrouding the land here and there in veils of falling snow, while elsewhere or through the snow itself the sun shone. Golden shadows, dazzling peaks, fairy tracery of branches against the blue summer sea! It was a day to Live,—and work could be forgotten.

So Rockwell and I explored the woods, at first reverently treading one path that the snow about us might still lie undisturbed. But soon the cub in the boy broke out and he rolled in the deepest thickets, shook the trees down upon himself, lay still in the snow for me to cover him completely, washed his face till it was crimson, and wound up with a naked snow-bath. I photographed him standing thus in the deep snow at the water's edge with the mountains far off behind him. Then he dried himself at the roaring fire we'd made ready and felt like a new boy—if that can be imagined. We both sketched out-of-doors for a little while in the morning like young lady amateurs. I tried it again two or three times throughout the day with indifferent results; it was too beautiful. We cut wood too, and that went with a zest. While Rockwell dried himself after his bath I searched in the woods for a Christmas tree and cut a fair-sized one at last for its top. Christmas is right upon us now. To-night the cranberries stew on the stove. *Olson has been here and has told us another part of his adven-*

tures. These stories seem to me so interesting as pictures of pioneering days that are already over that I shall continue to note them down as I hear them from him. Olson, in the early winter of 1886-7 left San Francisco for Juneau, Alaska, with his partner John—, a Norwegian, Louis Brown, who had attached himself to Olson's party and a man named Tom Boswell. They had met Boswell somewhere in San Francisco flashing a treasury receipt for $7,000 in gold which he claimed to have panned out in Alaska. Boswell knew the country and knew where gold was to be found and the party followed his lead. From Juneau this party and numberless other prospectors were carried by steamer to Chilkoot, a few miles below the present site of Skagway [?]. From here began the hard trip overland to the headwaters of the Yukon River. Every man hauled his outfit on a long sled and the outfits weighed from five hundred to a thousand pounds each. Olson's party was the second to get started; the first consisted of two men, Carter and Mahon, and their trail Olson followed to the Hootalinkwa River itself where they were finally all to carry on their operations. The trail was difficult. The first twenty-five miles to Lake Lindeman involved an ascent over a pass that carried them above the timber line. The loads had to be packed over, a man carrying at one time about fifty pounds, though one huge Frenchman, whom they called Napoleon, carried as well three sacks of floor, one hundred and fifty pounds. On the descent from the pass Olson's party's sleds broke from them and raced down the mountain side overturning at last and doing some damage. Olson described a drink that was brewed that night after the recovery of their sleds and outfits, a drink for tired men, the best he had ever tasted. It contained a whole 50 cent bottle of Patent Pain Killer! From Lake Lindeman they continued with the main body of travellers through Mills Canyon, but from here bore off to the eastward following the lead of Carter and Mahon; and from here onward these two parties are alone on the trail to the head of the Hootalinkwa River. Carter endeavored to discourage Olson's party from following, for miners who know of the location of gold naturally would keep it to themselves. But they were not to be dissuaded. It seemed to Olson's crowd that men would not return to ground they had already worked upon without good cause. Three or four days journey from the river of their destination both parties cached provisions. On the river they separated and began prospecting the bay for float gold. Of Boswell, Olson's party was by now heartily sick. It appeared that he had come almost provisionless having but a 25 pound sack of flour and some bacon. He sponged upon the others and began to appear to Olson a thorough rascal. He left them and went up stream while Olson and the two others followed it down. These men were all without experience. Olson was the only miner but the conditions here were new to him. John was a trapper and both he and Olson carried with them a full equipment of traps. Louis had been a fisherman and a goose herd. They had little luck. At last they overtook Carter and Mahon. These allowed Olson to pan out a prospect they had tried and seeing his results told him it would yield $8.00 a day. That was about all the party had counted on and they were half inclined to hold that prospect with the others had relinquished. However they finally continued down the river travelling on the ice. But they were not rid of Boswell. One day he appeared racing down behind them on the river's other shore. He travelled abreast of his former companions hoping it appeared to be asked to rejoin them. At last, prospecting a bar on his side, he set up a shout. Waving his hat he called, "Come on, boys, we've struck it rich." They went over. It was fairly good, yielding probably $16.00 a day. Boswell would share it with them but he demanded a larger than proportionate share. This the others would not yield. "If you stake this claim," finally said Olson, "we'll move on. If you don't stake it we will; but make up your mind." He held it and the others continued down. They were behind Carter and Mahon yielding them, who had been there before, the first privileges. They presently found a small but good bar that Louis staked and later another that was held by John. Then they had reached traces of the last year's work of Carter and Mahon and returned up stream prospecting for another claim. They reached Boswell's claim and he joined them. "Look here boys," he said, "there are four of us and only three claims, but let's work them together and share alike. To be sure I have no grub but since one of us has no claim let the man who can best handle a boat go down the river in the spring and bring up grub." That was himself for in a boat or canoe he was an expert. They set to work. Olson with a whip saw ripped out lumber, planed it with a little block plane he'd brought along, and built a river boat. Nails they had none, so from the sleds' runners he cut nails and they answered well. Gold as yet they had taken out none. One day there appeared on the river three newcomers. The "Montana Boys" they were and Boswell knew them. He shouted his great "Hurra." "Come on over, I've struck it fine," he said, and you shall share. "What do you mean by that?" said Olson. "We have nothing to do with them" "I told them," said

Boswell, "that whatever I found I'd share with them" "Well then you'll have to choose between us," said Olson—and Boswell went to the Montana Boys. They camped near together, both parties, and began to make their rockers. Boswell, who was the expert, would tell the others nothing but Olson copied him stick by stick and ended with a proper rocker and moreover better made than the others and neatly planed. Boswell and the Montana Boys beginning work in Boswell's claim Olson and his party went to their lower claim, that of Louis. Finishing there they returned up stream of John's—and found it robbed. Boswell and his crowd had stolen it and cleaned it out and then turned up stream. For a moment follow Boswell and his immediate fortunes. They presently came to Carter and Mahon working clumsily with hatchets to hew out lumber for a rocker. "Don't do that," said Boswell, "go down to the claim we've left. You'll find slabs there that we've sawed out. With these you can make a job of your rocker." The two accepted what was offered and went in their canoe down stream to Boswell's claim. Then they hewed off the rough sides of the slabs, loaded them and returned. The trip took them four days. On their return their claim had been stripped and Boswell and the rest had gone. Of this Olson learned on meeting with Carter on returning for his cache. Carter was amazed at learning that Olson knew nothing of Boswell. "He's the greatest rascal in Alaska. The money he took out last year he stole from his partners on the Stewart river!" Olson, John and Louis continued on the river. Their provisions lasted well. With a fish hook made of a sled runner Olson caught some large pike. John shot two bear cubs in an exciting adventure in which, while escaping up a tree in fear of the bear mother, he discovered himself accompanied there by the two cubs, hidden in the foliage above him. He shot them and finally descended the tree, took a dead cub in each hand and in a panic of fear raced home for camp. Now they're bound up stream again. The current is swift and the boat is heavy with the outfit and a moose they'd killed for meat. Olson in the boat manages here in the current while Louis and John pull on the tow-line ashore. Louis scoffs at Olson—they are not friends—and Olson bids him try the boat. At a bend in the river the current eddies against a jam of logs. The boat under Louis' hands is thrown against it and in an instant overturned. (Here Olson whispered solemnly, "If I'd had a gun I'd have shot that fellow then!") Tied to the boat were Olson's gun, the shot-gun and Olson's blanket. These contained also the gold. Everything else had gone. From the stream two more guns were rescued, a partially used sack of flour and a sack of oatmeal. They were miles upon miles in the wilderness and foodless. There was but one thing to do. Race down the river to the Yukon and continuing on that river reach Forty Mile, the nearest settlement; and more than three hundred miles away. Carter and Mahon gave them a little sugar, flour and salt as they passed—more they could not themselves spare—and they continued. One night Olson was awakened by a splash in the river. He and John followed a gleaming wake in the darkness, finally shot at it, and heard the thrashing of a great creature. Hastily everything was packed into the boat and they embarked on the dark river. They overtook the dead creature, a moose, tied a line to it and from the swift current sought for a landing place. In shoal water they all sprang overboard and hauled the moose and the boat ashore. There in the shoal water they skinned and cut up the beast and, still in darkness, camped on that shore for the rest of the night. The moose meat was a godsend. But it soon began to spoil. From some Indians on the way they procured salt and cured what was left and traded for two 75 pound king salmon. And Forty Mile was reached! There were hungry men. They had little to share, for themselves they lived on but one meal a day. Olson had however one thing that they had not—tobacco—and it was shared to its end. All waited for the return of the little river steamers and the year's provisions and all must wait till fall. Now came Carter and Mahon and joined the colony at Forty Mile. And at last one day word was brought in that Boswell, his brother George Boswell and McCloud, one of the Montana Boys, had come and camped a mile or two above the settlement. That night Carter loaded his double barrel gun with buck-shot and went up the river to Boswell's camp. He waited near there till morning, but Boswell and the rest had fled. It was learned later that on the Boswell party being joined by George Boswell they had gone to the lake at the head of the Hootalinkwa River. Then Boswell, McCloud and George had rolled the other Montana Boys of their gold and, taking the only boat, fled to Forty Mile. From there they fled as has been told. They went down stream and were next heard of at Nuklukyet. Coming there they brought a great quantity of provisions from Fredericks the store keeper and retired to a small island in midstream to live. They built them-selves a cabin and procured a native woman for companionship. Presently some of the miners from Forty Mile reached Nuklukyet. They learned of Boswell's deal with Fredericks, the store keeper, and on asking to see it were shown the "gold dust" given to him by Boswell. It was a preposterous mixture of copper and quicksilver, with gold to color it. A miners meeting was held and Boswell was notified to make good. "Mind your own business," he replied, and made his cabin ready for a siege. He chinked it thoroughly on the outside and cut loopholes. But the miners were not to be bluffed and gave him a time limit to yield or be attacked—and he yielded. Returning to his cabin the crowd continued there until early spring. By then all were filthy with disease and George Boswell was near death. The elder brother, McCloud and another man—whom Olson believes to have been his one time partner Louis Brown, who during the winter had left Forty Mile,—fled down stream in a boat. They reached Russian Mission, crossed the portage to the Kuskokwim river, stayed here some time and finally, procuring a sloop, cruised with no good purpose in Bering Sea. Boswell finally reached Unalaska and from there took the steamer for Alaska. Olson saw him in Seattle ten years later. He had by then a wooden leg and operated an "information bureau" for Prospectors. He was known then as "Peg Leg Tom." He lost his leg in his Bering Sea cruise, chewed off by a polar bear and amputated cleanly at Unalaska's hospital—not, as he claimed himself, by his own hand. Once more he returned to Alaska as the guide for a party of prospectors. He took them to Boswell's Bar, "Peg Leg Bar" is has become. There was little gold left then in the Stewart River. Somewhat discredited, he tried to help his fortunes by robbing the Indian caches. He was detected and fled reaching and passing through Dawson but three days before an Indian reached there to put the mounted police on his trail. And that is all that Olson knows of Boswell.

At Forty Mile Olson and John wintered, prospecting a little but halted in this by Olson's scurvy. Of 117 men at Forty Mile that winter 26 had scurvy. "Napoleon" the giant Frenchman among them, and these died. In the spring Olsen came down the river in the steamer. At Nuklukyet it was proposed to put the convalescent George Boswell aboard but the miners vowed they'd throw him into the river if 'twas done. George Boswell later made his way to St. Michael. It was thought to hold him there for trial but evidence was lacking to convict him. Of Olson's arrival at San Francisco in 1888 it has already been told.

Friday, December Twentieth
The beautiful snow is fast going under the falling rain! With only five

126

Cain

more days before Christmas it is probable we'll have little if any snow on the ground then. A snowless Christmas in Alaska!

This day was as uneventful as could be. Part of the morning was consumed in putting a new handle into the sledge hammer. It was too dark to paint long, really hardly an hour of daylight. These days slip by so easily and with so little accomplished! Only by burning midnight oil can much be done.

SUNDAY, DECEMBER TWENTY-SECOND

Both yesterday and to-day it has poured rain. They've not been unpleasant days, however. Occasional let-ups have allowed us to cut wood and get water without inconvenience. This morning Olson, fearing that a continuance of the mild weather would melt the ice in the lake and send his bags of fish to the bottom, went out to the center of the lake where they hung suspended through a hole in the ice and brought them in. But so precarious has the ice become that he carried a rope and took me along in case of trouble. To get out upon the ice we had to go some distance along the lake's shore.

Returning we missed meeting Rockwell who had gone to join us. Not for some time did it occur to me to call him. It was well I did call. The poor boy on not seeing us had suddenly concluded we were drowned. A strip of water separated him from the ice. He was on the point of wading into this at the moment I called him. He was still terribly excited when he reached us.

Both days I have been occupied with humble, housewifely duties,—baking, washing, mending, and now the cabin is adorned with our drying clothes. Here where water must be carried so far it is the wet days that are wash days. Darning is a wretched nuisance. We should have socks enough to tide us over our stay here. Last night after Rockwell had been put to bed I sat down and did two of the best drawings I have made. At half past twelve I finished them, and then to calm my elation a bit for sleep read in the "Odyssey." At this my second reading of the book it's as intensely interesting—or more so—than before. As a story it is incomparably better than the "Iliad." To me it is full of suggestions for wonderful pictures.

Ten days from now it comes due for Olson to go to Seward. If only then we have mild, calm weather! But as yet we have seen no steamer go to Seward since early in the month. It looks as if the steamship com-

Superman

panies had combined to deprive Alaska of its Christmas mail and freight in a policy of making the deadlock with the government over the mail contracts intolerable. Meanwhile, instead of serving us, the jaunty little naval cruisers that summered here in idleness doubtless loaf away the winter months in comfortable southern ports. That, *at least, is a disgrace; and the sooner we're unburdened of that useless, inefficient body the better.*

Monday, December Twenty-third

Up to this morning the hard warm rain continued, and now the stars are all out and it might be thought a night in spring. At eight-thirty I walked over in sneakers and underwear for a moment's call on Olson, but he had gone to bed. And now although we'll have no snow the weather is fair for Christmas.

If Olson believes, as he says, that Christmas will pass as any other day he is quite wrong. The tree waits to be set up and it will surely be a thing of beauty blazing with its many candles in this somber log interior. I've given up the idea of dressing Olson as Santa Claus in goat's wool whiskers. Santa Claus without presents would move us to tears. There are a few little gifts,—a pocketknife and a kitchen set of knife, fork, and can-opener for Olson. An old broken fountain pen for Rockwell, some sticks of candy,—and the dinner! What shall it be? Wait!

It is midnight. I've just finished a good drawing. The lamp is about at its accustomed low mark—yesterday it had to be filled twice! Those nights when without a clock I sat up so late and to so uncertain an hour I have discovered by the lamp and clock together to have been really long. My bedtime then was after two or three o'clock—but I arose later. To-day I finished a little picture for Olson and so did Rockwell. These were forgotten in my list of presents as I've just written it. I have shown in my picture the king of the island himself striding out to feed the goats while Billy, rearing on his hind legs, tries to steal the food on the way. Rockwell's picture is of Olson surrounded by all the goats in a more peaceful mood. Olson's cabin is in the background. I wish we had more to give the good old man. At any rate he dines with us.

Christmas Eve!

We've cleaned house, stowed everything away upon shelves and hooks and in corners, moved even my easel aside; decorated the roof timbers with

Olsen, and just as they approach the cabin
the door opens wide and fairyland is
revealed to them. It is wonderful. The
interior of the cabin is illuminated as never
before, as no cabin interior perhaps ever was
among these wild mountains. Then all aglow

and smiling those two children come in.
Who knows which was the more entranced.
Then Olsen and I drink solemnly a
beautiful toast and the old man says: "I'd
give everything, yes, everything I have in the
world to have your wife here now!" And
now the presents are handed out. For
Olsen, his picture, from Rockwell. Ah, he

131

dense hemlock boughs, stowed quantities of wood behind the stove—
for there must be no work on that holiday—and now both Rockwell and
I are in a state of suppressed excitement over to-morrow.

What a strange thing! Nothing is coming to us, no change in any respect
in the routine of our lives but what we make ourselves,—and yet the day
looms so large and magnificent before us! I suppose the greatest festivals
of our lives are those at which we dance ourselves. You need nothing from
outside,—not even illusion. Certainly children need to be given scarcely
an idea to develop out of it an atmosphere of mystery and expectation as
real and thrilling to themselves as if it rested upon true belief.

Well, the tree is ready, cut to length with a cross at the foot to stand
upon, and a cardboard and tin-foil star to hang at its top. And now as to
Christmas weather. This morning, as might just as well have been
expected, was again overcast. Toward evening light snow began to fall.
It soon turned to rain and the rain now has settled down to a gentle, even,
all-night-and-day pace. Let it snow or rain and grow dark at midday! The
better shall be our good Christmas cheer within. This is the true Christmas land. The day should be dark, the house further overshadowed by
the woods, tall and black. And there in the midst of that somber, dreadful
gloom the Christmas tree should blaze in glory unrivaled by moon or
sun or star.

CHRISTMAS DAY ON FOX ISLAND

It is mild; the ground is almost bare and a warm rain falls. First the Christmas tree all dripping wet is brought into the house and set upon its feet.
It is nine feet and a half high and just touches the peak of the cabin. There
it stands and dries its leaves while Rockwell and I prepare the feast.

Both stoves are kept burning and the open door lets in the cool air.
Everything goes beautifully; the wood burns as it should, the oven heats,
the kettle boils, the beans stew, the bread browns in the oven just right,
and the new pudding sauce foams up as rich and delicious as if instead
of the first it were the hundredth time I'd made it. And now everything
is ready. The clock stands at a quarter to three. Night has about fallen and
lamp light is in the cabin.

"Run, Rockwell, out-of-doors and play awhile." Quickly I stow the
presents about the tree, hang sticks of candy from it, and light the candles.

Rockwell runs for Mr. Olson, and just as they approach the cabin the
door opens and fairyland is revealed to them. It is wonderful. The interior

MENU

Fox Island, Christmas
1918

+ Hors d'œuvres +

Olives

Pickles

+ Entree +

Spaghetti a la Fox Island

+ Roti +

Beans a la Resurrection Bay

Murphies en Casserole

Cranberry Sauce

+ Dessert +

Plum Pudding Magnifique

Sauce a la Alaska Rum

Demi Tasse

Nuts   Raisens   Bon-bons

Home Sweet Home Cider

+

Music by the German Band.

of the cabin is illuminated as never before, as perhaps no cabin interior ever was among these wild mountains. Then all amazed and wondering those two children come in. Who knows which is the more entranced?

Then Olson and I drink in deep solemnity a silent toast; and the old man says, "I'd give everything—yes everything I have in the world—to have your wife here now!"

And the presents are handed out. For Olson this picture from Rockwell. Ah, he thinks it's wonderful! Then for Rockwell this book—a surprise from Seward. Next for Olson a painting, a kitchen set, and a pocketknife. By this time he's quite overcome. It's the first Christmas he has ever had! And Rockwell, when he is handed two old copies of the "Geographic Magazine" cries in amazement, "Why I thought I was to have no presents!" But he gets besides a pocketknife and the broken fountain pen and sits on the bed looking at the things as if they were the most wonderful of gifts.

Dinner is now set upon the table. Olson adjusts his glasses and reads the formal menu that lies at his place.

So we feast and have a jolly good time.

It is a true party and looks like one. Rockwell and I are in clean white shirts, Olson is magnificent in a new flannel shirt and his Sunday trousers and waistcoat. He wears a silk tie and in it a gold nugget pin. He is shaven, and clipped about the ears. How grand he looks! *All this might not have been done but that Rockwell had said to me the night before rather anxiously after he had lain some time in his bed, "Mr. Olson is going to dress up for Christmas, isn't he?"* The food is good and plentiful, the night is long, only the Christmas candles are short-lived and we extinguish them to save them for another time. Finally as the night deepens Olson leaves us amid mutual expressions of delight in each other's friendship, and Rockwell and I tumble into bed.

The next day and the next it is mild, resting—the weather seems to be—at this peaceful holiday season. We cut no wood and do little work. We write long letters, both of us, and consume at meal-time the food left over from Christmas. I read the "Odyssey," great story! Just now I am past that magnificent slaughter of the wooers, else these delayed pages would still be unwritten. A few more Odysseys to read here in this wild place and one could forget the modern world and return in manners and speech and thought to the heroic age. That would be an adventure worth trying! Maybe we are not so deeply permeated with the culture of to-day

The North Wind

that we could not throw it off. Surely the spirit of the heroes strikes home to our hearts as we read of them in the ancient books. *Now as I write it is*

SATURDAY, DECEMBER TWENTY-EIGHTH

For the first time in days the sun has risen in a clear sky and shone upon the mountains across from us. It is colder for ice has formed again on the tub of water out-of-doors. But there is a little wind.

I am writing in preparation for Olson's trip. He too is making ready. Food for the foxes is on the stove for many days' feeding, his engine gets a little burnishing—it's no insignificant voyage to Seward in the winter. If only it holds out fair and calm until a steamer comes! There's the hitch now. We have seen none go to Seward since the first of the month.

To-morrow probably the Christmas tree must come down. The hemlock trimmings shed all over the cabin till to-day I tore them out. Last night we had our final lighting of the tree. Rockwell and I stood out-of-doors and looked in at it. What a marvelous sight in the wilderness. If only some hapless castaways had strayed in upon us lured by that light! We sang Christmas carols out there in the dark, did a Christmas dance on the shore, and then came in and while the tree still burned told each other stories. Rockwell's story was about the adventures of some children in the woods, full of thrilling climaxes. It came by the yard. I told him of an Indian boy who longing for Christmas, went out into the dark woods at night and closed his eyes. And how behind his closed eyes he found a world rich in everything the other lacked. There was his Christmas tree and to it came the wild animals. They got each a present, the mother porcupine a box of little silken balls to stick onto her quills for decoration, and the father porcupine a tooth brush because his large teeth were so very yellow. After the story it was bedtime. Well . . . this fair day has passed, and with the night have come clouds and a cold gloom foreboding snow. But I have learned to expect nothing of the weather but what it gives us.

SUNDAY, DECEMBER TWENTY-NINTH

Squirlie's birthday party. Squirlie is seated in a condensed milk box. At his back hangs a brown sweater. About him stand his presents consisting chiefly of feathers. The table is spread with the feast in shells and the whole is brilliantly illuminated by a Christmas tree candle. Long life to Squirlie and may he never fall to pieces nor be devoured by moths!

. QUIRLIES BIRTHDAY PARTY .

Sunday December 29th. Fox Island.

Nothing of importance to-day but
what is pictured above. Squirlie is
seated in a condensed milk box. At
his back hangs a home sweater. Atms
him stand his presents consisting
chiefly of feathers. The table is spread
with the feast and the whole is
brilliantly illuminated by a Christmas tree
candle. Long life to squirlie, and
may he never fall to pieces nor
be devoured by marties!

Yesterday it rained gently, to-day it pours. I sit here with the door open and the stove slumbering—such weather in this country that the world believes to be an iceberg! But in Seward and on the mountains no doubt it is snowing enough. To-day I made so good a drawing that I'm sitting up as if the flight of time and the coming of morning were no concern of mine. It is half-past twelve!

New Year's Eve! Tuesday. This the tenth anniversary of Rockwell's parents and I have kept it as well as I could, working all day upon a drawing for his mother and to-night holding a kind of song service with Rockwell. Rockwell, who at nine years has every reason to celebrate to-day, however he may feel at twenty-nine, has written his mother a sweet little letter. I'm terribly homesick to-night and don't know what to say about it in these genial pages. It has been a solemn day.

When Olson was here to-night I began from playing the flute to sing. He was delighted and I continued. What a strange performance here in the wilderness, a little boy, and old man, listening as I sing loudly and solemnly to them without accompaniment. Olson brought us a pan of goat's milk to-day, as he often does. I make junket of it and it is a truly delicious dish, ever so much better than when made of cow's milk. It resembles a jelly of pure cream.

It has rained hard most of the day. At times a mist has hung in a band halfway up the mountain's height across the bay. It is a remarkable sight. To-night is as warm as any night in spring or autumn. It thaws continually and even the ice that once covered the ground beneath the snow is fast disappearing. The year goes out without a steamer having been seen to come with the Christmas mail.

It is close to midnight. I have one secret resolution to make for the new year and, that I may make it as earnestly and as truly as possible, the stars and the black sky shall be my witness. And so with the year nineteen hundred and eighteen I end this page.

IX. NEW YEAR

To Rockwell who asked what happened on the New Year that everybody sat up to see it come we tried hard to tell all sorts of yarns about explosions and rumblings, but he wouldn't believe a bit of it. He might have said, "How can anything like that happen here where nothing ever comes from the sky except rain?"

So far the new year is just exactly like the old's latter end but that it is more joyous. And the joy came at eleven-thirty P.M. of January first, gliding by about two miles out in the bay, a dazzle of lights like a fairy citadel, the STEAMER! At my cry Rockwell sat up in bed and gazed too. Olson unfortunately was in bed and we did not call him. So I set at once to work writing, tying up parcels, making lists, until two o'clock of this morning.

At eight we had Olson out of bed. I hung about there threatening him, ordering him, begging him to hurry. Old men are hard to move fast. He shaved standing up there in his cabin with the door wide open and the goats playing about him. I let him have a bite of breakfast, but not much. The dory had to be unbound—for we tie them to the ground—and turned right-side up, and loaded and launched,—but all that only after half an hour's cranking of the engine, the infernal things! It would look like snow one minute and be fair the next; but it held fair enough finally for Olson to get off and disappear—to our immense joy. He laughs at our eagerness to get him off for the mail.

Yesterday was Olson's day for celebrating and many times we drank to the New Year together. But I would work, to his disgust. Still he understands pretty well the strange madness that possesses me, and is not at all unsympathetic. I explained to him one day the difference between working to suit yourself and working to suit other people. He'd defy the world at any time he chose no matter how poor his fortunes.

Well, now we wait for mail. Already I'm impatient for Olson's return and that cannot well be before the day after to-morrow. Rockwell and I walked around the bay in the afternoon more to have a look toward Seward where our mail comes from than for anything else. But Seward was hidden in falling snow. All the bay was shrouded in mist and snow. But our own cove was beautiful to look back upon with its white peaks and dark forest, and far down at the water's edge our tiny cabins from one of which the thick smoke of the smoldering fire curled upwards.

SUNDAY, JANUARY FIFTH

Olson is still away. It is wearing to wait this way in hope,—for we will hope even if the wind blows and the snow falls. And so it has done. The day following Olson's departure it was wonderfully fair and calm, but the next day, it being the day he should have returned, a heavy snowstorm set in. And to-day with less snow there was more wind,—not so much that he could not have come but enough that he didn't. We walked down the beach and scanned the bay with the glasses, and up to dark I looked continually for the little boat to be rounding the headland.

It seems as if that were all the news, but the days have really been full of work and other interest. The snow itself, lying deep and light and over all—even the tree tops—is a delight. Rockwell and I played bear and hunter today tracking each other in the woods. Only the goats are miserable these days with their browse all covered but what they can gnaw from the tree trunks. Billy at this season is a fury. One has really to go armed with a clout. Yesterday he burst in the door of Olson's shed and then inside managed to shut the door on himself. When I investigated the strange banging that I'd been hearing for some time, I found him. He had even piled things against the door. While no actual damage has been done he has tossed every blessed thing about with his horns. Boxes, pails, sacks of grain, cans, rope, tools, all lie piled in confusion about the floor. It does no good to beat the creature. He will learn nothing. It is about one-thirty A. M. I've written more than I intended writing. My heart is set upon the mail and nothing else.

140

Another of Rockwell's Drawings

Monday, January Sixth

With Olson still away and the mail with him what can there be to report. It snows. It is so mild that we walk about hatless, coatless, mittenless. Drip, drip, drip, goes it from the eaves continuously. The snow has fallen from the trees. On the ground it lies deep and heavy. Tomorrow maybe we shall take to snowshoes. Rockwell and I each took a trip along the beach to look for Olson. As I stood there peering into the haze toward Seward a head arose from the water close to me. It was a seal. He looked all about him for the greatest while, went under, reappeared again near by once more, and then was gone. Billy burst open that shed of Olson's again. Some day I shall murder a goat!

Wednesday, January Eighth

Two more days and Olson still away. I'm furious at him. Yesterday he could well have come, to-day it has been impossible. We seem to do little here but wait. Even at the height of to-day's storm I found myself continually going to the little window to look for a boat. Rain and snow, rain and snow! Ah, if only we had our mail here—then these warm, white days would be delightful. Yesterday we wore our snowshoes for the first time, but only to tramp down the cove and look toward Seward.

The only recompense for Olson's absence is Nanny's milk. I'm an expert milker now and can do the job before she finishes her cup of oats. I have to, for at the finish she leaps madly to escape me. Goat's milk junket and orange marmalade; sublime!

Friday, January Tenth

One hour ago it was as beautiful a moonlit night as one ever beheld. The softest veils of cloud passed the moon and cast over the earth endlessly varied, luminous shadows. The mountain tops, trees, rocks, and all, are covered with new snow; the valleys and the lower levels are black where rain has cleared the trees. It is so beautiful here at times that it seems hard to bear. And now at this moment the rain falls as if it had fallen for all time and never would cease. Oh Olson, Olson! Is it anything to you in your old age to be so madly wanted? Here it truly is conceivable that any condition of bad weather could visit us for months without relief. There seems no rhyme or reason to it until you see it as the reverse of marvelously fair weather; a blue sky is here as wrong as rain in a rainless desert land.

Nothing has happened. I am making good drawings and have made

Weltschmerz

two small woodcuts. Billy to-day again tackled the door of Olson's shed. My fixing of the lock proved too good. That held—while he burst the door to pieces. I caught him at the finish of it; I become a maniac at such a time. I pursued the beast with a club in a mad chase through the heavy snow, catching him often enough to get some satisfaction at least in the beating I gave him. He fears me now and that's something gained. But it's a bad matter both for Billy and for me.

It is now after midnight and I've just finished a drawing. Rockwell is concerned about these late hours and when I told him that I could work so very well alone at night he seriously suggested that I send him out in the daytime to stay all day without dinner so that I could work better. I'm reading about King Arthur and the round table to him; that's good for both of us. He has made himself a lance and a sword and to-morrow I expect to confer some sort of knighthood upon him. Apropos of the book of King Arthur, Rockwell said to-day, "I don't think the pictures in the book are half nice enough. I think of a wonderful picture when you read the story and then when I see the one in the book I'm disappointed." And these King Arthur pictures are rarely good in execution. It just shows that one need not attempt to palm off unimaginative stuff, much less trash, on children. The greatest artists are none too good to make the drawings for children's books. Imagination and romance in pictures and stories a child asks for above all, and those qualities in illustration are the rarest.

Monday, January Thirteenth

Of the three days that have again passed two have been quite fair enough for Olson to have come. Both yesterday and to-day Rockwell and I made frequent trips down the shore to look for him. It is terribly depressing to have your heart set upon that mail that doesn't come. I begin to think that some other cause than the weather holds Olson away. It is possible that the steamer we saw going to Seward was no mail steamer, and that Olson, who has gone for his pension money, is waiting for a mail. I feel like making no record of these days. I take pleasure only in their quick passage.

Saturday night Rockwell received the order of knighthood. For three quarters of an hour he stayed upon his knees watching over his arms. He was all that time as motionless as stone and as silent. Now he is Sir Lancelot of the Lake and jousts all day with imaginary giants and wicked knights. He has rescued one queen for himself but as yet none for me.

We have run about some on our snowshoes, though the snow is nowhere deep enough for that except along the shore. The weather is still mild—hardly freezing at all—and it forever successively rains, snows, and hails. All the animals are still alive. I don't love them, they're rather a nuisance. Nothing could be less amusing than a blue fox,—small creatures, excessively timid, of cowed demeanor. Saturday I had to get a bag of fish from the lake where they had been soaking and cook up another great supply of fox food.

Wednesday, January Fifteenth

Yesterday to begin with a snowstorm and then a clear, gray day. To-day blue sky in the morning, a north wind and bitter cold; gray again at noon and mild. By the geological survey report of Kenai Peninsular, January should average in temperature at Seward sixteen degrees. From now on it must average close to zero to give us sixteen for the month. Here it's not as cold as New York. Rockwell bathed to-night standing within six feet of the open door. I have definitely decided that Olson stays for some cause other than the weather, although to-day and yesterday he could not have come. We snowshoed a bit to-day. Alaska snowshoes are certainly the easiest that ever were to travel on.

Thursday, January Sixteenth

Well, after to-day there remains no doubt that Olson stays away purposely—unless he's sick or dead. Rockwell's theory that Seward has been totally swept away by a terrible fire, with every man, woman, and child of its inhabitants, I disproved to-night. We walked down the beach and there were the lights of the great city brighter it seemed than ever. Either there has been no mail boat at all since early in December or there has been no mail from Juneau whence Olson's "check-que," as he calls it, comes. Well it profits us nothing to speculate on this.

The day has been glorious, mild, fair, with snow everywhere even on the trees. The snow sticks to the mountain tops even to the steepest, barest peaks painting them all a spotless, dazzling white. It's a marvelous sight. Rockwell and I journeyed around the point to-day and saw the sun again. To-night in the brilliant moonlight I snowshoed around the cove. There never was so beautiful a land as this! Now at midnight the

Victory

moon is overhead. Our clearing seems as bright as day,—and the shadows are so dark! From the little window the lamplight shines out through the fringe of icicles along the eaves, and they glisten like diamonds. And in the still air the smoke ascends straight up into the blue night sky.

Saturday, January Eighteenth

Two beautiful days, these last. And to-night the wind blows and the snow falls and it is very cold. The days are uneventful. We journey many times down the beach over our snowshoe trail. That's our out-of-doors diversion,—to look up the bay toward Seward. But the view is beautiful. Loftier mountains, more volcano shaped are about Seward, and they're dazzling white.

Yesterday Rockwell found otter tracks crossing from the salt water to the lake,—a lot of them. It's wonderful to think that those fine creatures have crossed the five long miles of water. Their footprints are as large as a good-sized dog's. They seem to have a great time frisking about as they travel. On one little slope they have made a slide. No footprints are there at all,—only the smoothly worn track. We see no wild life as a rule but the eagles. They're all about in plenty, magnificent birds when seen close to, and when flying at the mountain's height still surprisingly large.

The milk goat is dry,—so that's one chore less. Rockwell feeds the goats every day, but I can't trust him with the foxes; he'd leave the door open as likely as not. (It was reserved for Olson himself to let this happen. May twenty-ninth he writes in a letter to me:

"Had a skear or acksedent on the eighteenth. i vas putteng som grase in to the fox Corrals an i most heav left the hok of van i turnd around the dor vas open and 1. fox goan the litle femall in the Corall naxst to the goat Hous. And the fox var over at the tant i cald to em et vas suppertam to Com bake and get som sepper and He sat down and luckt at me bot finly mosed of op in the Hill. i take the other fox and put em in the other Corall and left the 2—tow Coralls open and put feed in the seam es nothing ad apen. the first night i did not sleep vary val. the sakond night and not show-ing up, bot naxst morning i Came out to the Corall the feed vas goin en the pan and the fox vas sleping on the box var he allves du and i felt a little Beatter van the doors ar shut.")

I'm hard at work painting by day and drawing at night. Twenty-five good drawings are done. On the fair, warm days Rockwell spends most of his time out-of-doors. Being Sir Lancelot still delights him and there's not a stump in the vicinity that has not been scarred by his attacks with lance and sword. These stumps are really mostly all giants. I am now reading the Department of Agriculture year book. It's very instructive.

Tuesday, January Twenty-first

The north wind rages to-night. It is cold and clear starlight. With the violent wind-gusts the snow sweeps by in clouds—sweeps by except for what sweeps in. Over my work table it descends in a fine, wet spray so that I've had to cover that place with canvas and work elsewhere. A wild day it has been and a wild night is before us. And yesterday was little brother to it.

These days are wonderful but they are terrible. It is thrilling now with Olson absent to reflect that we are absolutely cut off from all mankind, that we cannot, in this raging sea, return to the world nor the world come to us. Barriers must secure your isolation in order that you may experience the full significance of it. The romance of an adventure hangs upon slender threads. A banana peeling on a mountain top tames the wilderness. Much of the glory of this Alaska is in the knowledge I have that the next bay—which I may never choose to enter—is uninhabited, that beyond those mountains across the water is a vast region that no man has ever trodden, a terrible ice-bound wilderness.

We begin to think less of Olson's return. I have settled to my work and can imagine things continuing as they are for weeks. They will continue so unless the wind forsakes the north. Two days ago after a very cold night we awoke to thunder and lightning—and snow! In two hours the sun was out. That afternoon I stripped and danced awhile in the snow—a little while. Then, after a hot bath, out again in my nakedness for a roll in the snow, dressed,—and felt a new man. Rockwell loves it all more and more. He seems absolutely contented and spends hours a day outdoors.

What a marvel is a child's imagination! It is a treat for Rockwell to play "man-eater" at bedtime and attack me furiously. And if at any time I'll just enter his pretend-world it's all he can wish for. Another filthy mess of fox-food has been prepared and a new sack of salt fish put to soak in the lake. I do hate that chore. Pioneering I relish; ranching I despise, at least blue fox ranching. The miserable things slink about so in such sick and mean spirited fashion.

148

Wilderness

149

Sometimes the smoke goes up the flue—and sometimes down. And that's not good for the fire. I sit within six inches of the stove with a frozen nose and icy feet. The wind sifts through the walls. Now, with our moss calking shrunken and dried and shriveled further with the cold, our cabin would be light without windows. These are so far the coldest days of winter. Although it blows straight from the north, whence only fair weather comes, the day is dark with drifting snow cloud high. The water of the bay is hidden in driving vapor. We cut wood and stuff it everlastingly into the stove. To-day seventy pieces for the ravenous air-tight, big chunks, have been cut and split—and we'll cut again to-morrow. But with all the trouble of cold weather we'd be mightily disappointed if the winter slipped by without it.

It's a real satisfaction to find that my calculations in supplies, in bedding, in heating equipment were just right for conditions here. We're running low now in cereals and milk but we planned to visit Seward this month to restock. Olson's absence is quite outside of all plans. If he isn't sick it's hard to explain reasonably in any way.

For the past three weeks I have made on an average no less than one good drawing a day, really drawings I'm delighted with. I've struck a fine stride and moreover a good system for my work here to continue upon. During the day I paint out-of-doors from nature by way of fixing the forms and above all the color of the out-of-doors in my mind. Then after dark I go into a trance for a while with Rockwell subdued into absolute silence. I lie down or sit with closed eyes until I "see" a composition,—then I make a quick note of it or maybe give an hour's time to perfecting the arrangement on a small scale. Then when that's done I'm care free. Rockwell and I play cards for half an hour, I get supper, he goes to bed. When he's naked I get him to pose for me in some needed fantastic position, and make a note of the anatomy in the gesture of my contemplated drawing. Little Rockwell's tender form is my model perhaps for some huge, hairy ruffian. It's great joke how I use him. Generally I have to feel for the bone or tendon that I want to place correctly.

Last night I drew, laughing to myself. A lion was my subject. I have often envied Blake and some of the old masters their ignorance of certain forms that let them be at times so delightfully, impressively naive. I've thought it matters not a bit how little you know about the living form provided you proceed to draw the thing according to some definite, con-

Zarathustra and his Playmates

sistent idea. Don't conceal your ignorance with a slur, be definite and precise even there. Well, by golly, this lion gave me my chance to be unsophisticated; such a silly, smirking beast as I drew! At last it became somewhat rational and a little dignified, but it still looks like a judge in a great wig. But a lion that lets a naked youth sleep in his paws as this one does may be expected to be a little unbeastly. When I began to write these pages to-night the stars were out. Now it snows or hails on the roof!

SATURDAY, JANUARY TWENTY-FIFTH

It is bitterly cold weather, as cold continuously as I've ever experienced. Both yesterday and to-day the wind has been exceptionally violent and the air full of flying snow. Both of Olson's water barrels—in the house— have frozen solid. One bulged and burst the bottom rolling itself off onto the floor.

SUNDAY, JANUARY TWENTY-SIXTH

A day of hard work with Rockwell in bed for a change. Just a little stomach upset—and he's all right now. Felled a tree and cut up fifteen feet of it, taking advantage of this glorious day. It was much milder than for days it has been and it still holds so to-night. There's no wind and that makes ever so much difference in the cabin. Now if it will hold calm and mild for a day we'll see whether or not Olson is yet ready to return.

TUESDAY, JANUARY TWENTY-EIGHTH

I'm reading "Zarathustra," "Write with blood, and thou wilt learn that blood is spirit." So that book was written. Last night I made a drawing of Zarathustra leading the ugliest man by the hand out into the night to behold the round moon and the silver waterfall. What a book to illustrate! The translator of it says that Zarathustra is such a being as Nietzsche would have liked himself to be,—in other words his ideal man. It seems to me that the ideal of a man is the real man. You are that which in your soul you choose to be; your most beautiful and cherished vision is yourself. What are the true, normal conditions of life for any man but just those perfect conditions with which he would ideally surround himself. A man is not a sum of discordant tendencies—but rather a being perfect for one special place; and this is Olson's creed.

My chief criticism of Zarathustra is his taste for propaganda. Why, after all, concern himself with the mob. In picturing his hero as a teacher has

Frozen Fall

153

not Nietzsche been tricked away from a true ideal to an historical one? Of necessity the great selfish figures of all time have gone down to oblivion. It's the will of human society that only the benefactors of mankind shall be cherished in memory. A pure ideal is to be the thing yourself, concerning yourself no bit with proving it. And if the onward path of mankind seems to go another way than yours—proud soul, let it.

Wednesday, January Twenty-ninth

Alaska can be cold! Monday broke all records for the winter. Tuesday made that seem balmy. It was so bitterly cold here last night in our "tight little cabin" that we had to laugh. Until ten o'clock when I went to bed the large stove was continuously red hot and running at full blast. And yet by then the water pails were frozen two inches thick—but ten feet from the stove and open water at supper time, my fountain pen was frozen on the table, Rockwell required a hot water bottle in bed, the fox food was solid ice, my paste was frozen, and that's all. My potatoes and milk I had stood near the stove. At twelve o'clock the clock stopped—starting again from the warmth of breakfast cooking. I put the water pail at night behind the stove close to it, and yet it was solid in the morning. We burn an unbelievable amount of wood, at least a cord a week in one stove. So I figure we earn a dollar a day cutting wood. We felled another tree to-day and cut most of it up. Still we manage to gain steadily with our wood pile always in anticipation of worse weather. Last night at sundown the bay appeared indescribably dramatic. Dense clouds of vapor were rising from the water obscuring all but a few peaks of the mountains and darkening the bay. But above the sun shone dazzlingly on the peaks and through the thinner vapor, coloring this like flames. It was as if a terrible fire raged over the bay. This morning for hours it was dark from clouds of vapor. They swept in over our land and coated the trees of the shore with white frost.

Yesterday I had to go to the lake and chop out a bag of fish for the foxes. I returned covered with ice and the fish were frozen solid before I reached the cabin. I cut them up to-day with the axe and cooked a week's supply of food for the foxes.

Rockwell has been a trump. The weather can't be too cold for him. This morning he pulled his end of the saw without rest. He rarely goes out now without his horse, lance, and sword and he addresses me always as "My Lord." Surely Lancelot himself was no gentler knight. And now

154

it continues. To increase our lead on the weather we set to work upon a twenty eight inch tree. We had to throw it somewhat against its natural lean and it was a terrible job. The wedge would not enter the frozen tree and when it at last did, nothing lifted the green mass that rested on it. Only after an hour's continuous

pounding with a heavy sledge-hammer, did I drive the wedge in to the head and only then did the tree fall. The face of one of these monsters — for to us they seem gigantic — is thrilling. This one fell just where we had aimed it, down a narrow avenue in the woods. Ripping and crashing it fell, carrying down a smaller tree in its limbs. Then Rockwell and I set to work with the saw. When the drums were split up we hauled them to the cabin on Olson's Yukon sled.

155

it's bedtime. The cold is less than last night but still I sit huddled at the stove. It is the bitter wind that makes the trouble.

Thursday, January Thirtieth

A splendid day of wood cutting. It was milder and quite windless in our cove, although in the bay there were whitecaps. A light snow had begun to fall by noon and it continues. To increase our lead on the weather we set to work upon a twenty-eight inch tree. We had to throw it somewhat against its natural lean and it was a terrible job. The wedge would not enter the frozen tree and when it at last did it wouldn't lift the great mass that rested on it. Only after an hour's continuous pounding with the heavy sledge-hammer did I drive the wedge in clear to the head, and then the great tree fell. The fall of one of these monsters—for to us they seem gigantic—is thrilling. This one went straight where we had aimed it, down a narrow avenue in the woods. Ripping and crashing it fell carrying down a smaller tree with its limbs. Then Rockwell and I set to work with the saw. When the drums were split we hauled them to the cabin on Olson's Yukon sled. And now our wood pile is a joyous sight, while within the cabin we have a whole, cold day's supply.

Last night just as I was going to bed Rockwell began to talk in his sleep about some wild adventure with his imaginary savages. I asked him if he were cold. "No, my lord," he murmured and slept on. Very fine barley soup to-day. Water in which barley had been boiled, two bouillon cubes, onions browned in bacon fat. Rockwell said it was the best yet.

Saturday, February First

Again the days are like spring. Yesterday began the thaw and to-day continues it with rain most of the time. So we've stayed within doors, Sir Lancelot and my lordship working here at our craft. I have just completed my second drawing for the day. One a day has been the rate for a month—but yesterday the spirit didn't work. But the news! A great, old tramp steamer entered yesterday. That must carry mail and freight and send Olson back to us. If only it were a regular liner I'd know for sure. It is possible this steamer has been chartered to relieve the situation. Well—the next fair, calm day will show.

Sunday, February Second

It's before supper. Rockwell, who has just run out-of-doors for a romp, calls at this moment that he has lost his slipper in the snow and is barefooted. Out-of-doors is to us like another room. Mornings we wash in the snow, invariably. And with a mug of water in hand clean our teeth out there—and this in the coldest weather. We scour our pots with snow before washing them, throw the dish water right out of the door, and generally are in and out all day. . . . It is surely nonsense to think that changes of temperature give men colds. Neither of us has had a trace of a cold this winter, we haven't even used handkerchiefs—only sleeves. Nor does it give one a cold to be cold. I've tried that often enough to know. And a variable climate has, too, nothing to do with it, for what variableness could exceed an Alaska winter. Colds, like bad temper and loss of faith, are a malady of the city crowd.

It rains—this moment, the next it will hail—and then snow. Sometime to-day the sun has shone, sometime the wind has blown, and for the rest been calm. Altogether it has been too uncertain for us to expect Olson. And now for the sour-dough hot cakes and supper. For Rockwell, barley, "the marrow of men."

Rockwell to-day asked me how kings earned their living. I said they didn't earn it—just got the people to give it to them.

"What's that," he said laughing, "some sort of a joke they play on the people?"

So I guess it takes education to appreciate privilege. Incidentally, the war must be over and the heroes, having proved by their might that might does not make right—or that it does? (!) now have doffed the soldier's uniform of glory for the little-honored clothes of toil.

Monday, February Third

We are in the second month of Olson's absence. To-day it stormed mostly; heavy snow in the morning. Through the thick of it we heard faintly a steamer whistle. It seemed to be receding, outward bound. At four o'clock while a light snow fell the lightning played merrily and thunder crashed. It is like this: snow for half an hour, then rain—silence and calm for a few minutes. Suddenly huge hailstones pelt the roof, for all the world like rocks. This lasts a few seconds, there's a fierce gust of wind showering ice and snow from the tree tops down upon us, again calm and silence—and the performance is ready to begin again.

Tuesday, February Fourth

It has been so changeable to-day that we are still uncertain of Olson's intentions. We snowshoed down the beach in the beautiful, soft, new snow so at least to have a look toward Seward. There lay the bay calm and beautiful—and spotless. The scale of things is so tremendous here that I've little idea how far we shall be able to see the little, bobbing boat when it does come.

We sawed a lot of wood to-day bringing our pile clear up into the gable peak. It becomes a mania seeing the pile grow. In quiet weather we cut to forestall the storm; in the storm we still cut to be well ahead for days that may be worse. It is beautifully mild now. On February first Rockwell brought in some budding twigs. The alders all seem to be in bud and some charming, red-stemmed shrubs as well. It is midnight and past. My drawing is finished, the stove is piled for the night, cereal and beans in place upon it, so—Good-night.

Wednesday, February Fifth

A beautiful snowstorm all the day and to-night, still and mild. Rockwell has been out in it all day dressed in my overalls and mittens. He plays seal and swims in the deep snow. We built a snow house together. It is now about seven feet in diameter inside and as cozy as can be. I'm sure Rockwell will want to sleep there when it's finished. A curtain of icicles hangs before our little window.

I have carefully figured the cost of our living here from the food bills, all of which I have kept. I have bought $114.82 worth of provisions. I still have on hand $19.10 worth. For one hundred and fifty days it has cost us sixty-four cents a day for two, or thirty-two cents each,—a little over ten cents a meal. This for the current high prices everywhere and additionally high in Alaska seems very reasonable living. The figures include the very expensive Christmas luxuries. *What Olsen has given us we returned in other foods. It has not been much at that.*

Friday, February Seventh

Yesterday, THE SUN! For how many days he might have been shining at us I don't know, for it has been cloudy. However at noon it was all over the ground about us and shining in at my window. What a joyous sight after months of shadow! To-night the sun at setting again almost reached us. And yesterday as if spring had already come we began the day with snow baths at sunrise. Ha! That's the real morning bath! And to-day again. We step out-of-doors and plunge full length into the deep snow, scour to the eastward. The snow lay in the woods there heavy and deep and heavenly beautiful. No breath of wind had disturbed it small trees loaded with snow till they had bent double made shapes like frozen fountains

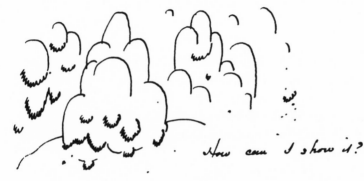

How can I show it?

Some little trees with branches starting far from the ground formed domed chambers about their stems.

From Inside.

159

our bodies with it, and rush back into the sheltering house and the red-hot stove. To Rockwell belongs all credit, or blame, for this madness. He will do it—and I'm ashamed not to follow. These two days have been cold and windy, north days,—but how beautiful! All of the day Rockwell plays out-of-doors swimming in the deep snow, now a seal, again a walrus. Gee, he's the great fellow for northern weather. Cooked the filthy fox mess yesterday, washed clothes to-day, sawed wood on both. Now it's twelve-thirty at night and I'm tired.

Saturday, February Eighth

All about me stand the drawings of my series, the "Mad Hermit." They look mighty fine to me. Myself with whiskers and hair! First, to-day, when the storm abated a bit, we sank a bag of fish in the lake and then started on snowshoes for the ridge to the eastward. The snow lay in the woods there heavy and deep. No breath of wind had touched it. The small trees, loaded, bent double making shapes like frozen fountains. Some little trees with their branches starting far from the ground formed with their drooping limbs domed chambers about their stems. Coming down it was great sport. We could slide down even in our sticky snowshoes. Rockwell, who was soaked through, undressed and spent the afternoon naked, playing wild animal about the cabin. Then at six-thirty we both had hot baths, and snow baths following. I begin to relish the snow bath. Rockwell was the picture of health and beauty afterwards with his rose-red cheeks and blue eyes.

Monday, February Tenth

Yesterday morning I bathed in a snowstorm, this morning it was too terribly, howlingly blusterous to run out into it. And now since one o'clock it is as calm and mild as it ever could be. Within the cabin it's even more cozy than usual. The snow is banked up against the big window to a third the window's height. By day the light seems curtained, by night doubly bright from reflected lamp-light. Heavy drifts are everywhere. Last night fine snow filtered in upon our faces as we slept but not enough to be uncomfortable. The cabin is fortunately placed as to drifts and our door-yard remains clear with a splendid bathing bank skirting it. Rockwell is at work now upon multiplication tables. He's a real student and is always seriously occupied with something in his hours indoors.

X. OLSON!

He returned last night, the eleventh of February, in a blaze of glory! Ah, the wonder of it and of all he brought. Rockwell and I sat at our cards just before supper-time. The day, a calm one, a fair one, had passed and Olson again had not come. We were downcast. Every possible cause for his continued absence had been reviewed in my mind. To wait longer was not to be endured. And so we sat with far-off thoughts and toyed with the silly cards. Suddenly the long, clear sound of a boat's horn reached us from the night outdoors. We ran and peered into the darkness. At last we saw a black spot moving far out on the water. Oh God! it was entering the cove. In what a frenzy of excitement we hurried down the beach! Nearer they come and nearer, men's voices, the little cabin light, and the vessel gliding toward us; they're abreast of us, they drop anchor. "Olson, Olson," I shout, "Olson, is that you?" "He's aboard," is answered, "How are you, and how's the little boy?" We see them loading a dory from the vessel's deck,—and now they row it to the shore. It's good to see a fine young fisherman and shake his hand. Again and once again the loads are ferried in and carried up the long and slippery low-tide beach. Rockwell has lighted Olson's lamp, he sweeps his cabin, and starts the fire in the stove. At the last load I slip aboard the vessel. I am "wanted." There stands Olson swaying gigantic on the deck above us as we bump the side. A bear's greeting! Olson is radiant, radiant and mellow with the joy of home-coming and the warmth of tasted spirits. The skipper I know, yes! the

161

good Englishman, Hogg, who had us once to dinner at his camp. Down in the cabin in the heat and fumes of a cooking feast we tip the friendly bottle.

Ah! tell me not, abstainer, of any glories you have known. One night, one midnight out on the black waters of a Newfoundland harbor, the million stars above, and on the wretched vessel's deck the horde of half-drunk, soul-starved men saying their passionate farewells,—on the dull plain of their life a flash of lightning revealed an abyss;—this night on the still, dark cove of Resurrection Bay, rimmed with wild mountains and the wilderness, strong men about you, mad, loosened speech and winged, prophetic vision,—God! but sane daylight seeing seems to touch but the white, hard surface of where life is hidden.

From the hot cabin I climbed the boat's ladder, up, up onto the world's heights. Ah, how the cold, clean wind from the wide spaces then swept my soul, and how close about my head the dome of heaven and the stars! This is no earth-ship but the deck of a meteor vessel that I tread, the moon ship of the ancient northern gods.

I row ashore for Rockwell, stow the goods higher on the beach, and we return aboard for supper. Over Rockwell the skipper makes a great fuss, says he's a famous oarsman and could beat his daddy, a fine, big, strong boy. Warm hearted skipper!—and he reaches again for the bottle and I drink. It's vinegar! Profuse apologies, and the right one is found.

We eat, we stuff!—and then the three us, Rockwell laden with presents of fruit, say good-night and row ashore. Poor, tired Olson, has little strength to move the heavy loads from the beach. No matter, I struggle alone and finally stow them in his cabin, a great pile. Then a cup of coffee with the old man, a little furious talk about the war,—fury at a world that could mess things so,—and home to bed where already Rockwell slept.

This morning the icy bath. Then without breakfast we began upon our mail. What a wonderful Christmas at last! The bed was piled high with presents, the table high with letters. We sorted and gloated like hungry tigers that in the ecstasy of possession merely lick their food. All through the morning and deep into the afternoon I read the mail. Unwashed dishes stood about, for meals we but ate what was at hand. (Here follows in the journal a list two pages long of presents, of books—what a shelf of them!—woollen clothes and sheepskin slippers, music for the flute, plum-pudding, candy, chocolate, cigarettes,—and ever so much more.) And that being about seven times as much as we've ever had before is all. Ah, in the wilderness you love your friends and they too think of you. Better than all, though, are the letters; such friendly letters never were before.

FRIDAY, FEBRUARY FOURTEENTH

The days go like the wind. So warm to-day and yesterday! We live out-of-doors. Now as I write the door stands open and the soft, moist, spring air enters to dispel the fumes of turpentine. I primed eight canvases to-day, six of which I had also stretched. This afternoon I painted at the northern end of the beach almost beneath a frozen waterfall, an emerald of huge size and wonderful form.

Rockwell is in high spirits. I think the augmentation of our diet brought by Olson's return will do him a lot of good. We had cut down on our use of milk to a can in two or three days. Now we may live on fish which Olson has in such quantities that we're to help ourselves. Olson has insisted on my accepting a fifty-pound sack of flour for my services during his six weeks' absence, and I expect to find it hard to be allowed to return the cereals that I am borrowing. What a contrast this free-handed country to the mean spirit of Newfoundland!

An amendment to the list of Christmas presents.

> *From Mother—a flannel shirt for R. and a book of fairy tales—a tiny one.*
> *From "Mother" Kathleen—some stuffed animals for R.*
> *From Mother—a box of colored crayons for R. He loves them.*
> Again All!

MONDAY, FEBRUARY SEVENTEENTH

Three days! and what has happened? I guess that on the first of them I stretched and painted canvas. On the second all day I painted out-of-doors, it was quite summer-like and the sun shone through diamond-dripping trees. And to-day I have written from early morning before breakfast until now, eleven at night. I have decided to go to Seward in a few days. It has become necessary to go back to New York very soon. I told Rockwell of this to-day and his eyes have scarcely been dry since. He has reasoned with me and inquired into every detail of the situation. He doesn't want to go to New York nor even to live in the country in the East. There'll be no ocean near nor any warm pond for bathing. And not even the thought that elsewhere he'd have playmates weighs against his love for this spot.

You should see Sir Lancelot now. His clothes are outgrown and outworn. They hang in tatters about him. His trousers are burst from the knee to the hip, his overalls that cover them are rags. His shirt is buttonless but for two in front. From above tattered elbows his sleeves hang in ribbons. His hair is long and shaggy; where it hung over his eyes I have cut it off short. But, his fair cheeks are as pink as roses, his eyes are beautiful and blue, his lips are red, and his face glows always with expression. So we don't care a rap for the rest—only Rockwell does! One day after he had regarded for a long time a certain unfortunate photograph of himself in which he looked like an idiot, he said, "Father, I'd like to dress up some day and put on my best clothes and brush my hair,—because I want to see if I really look like I do in this picture." Rockwell loves to look well and it's a real treat for him to dress up. So, that being the case and his tidy nature being so well assured I don't trouble a bit to adorn him. He cleans his teeth regularly and likes to do it. Mornings we get up together and go through a set of Dr. Sargent's exercises, do them with great energy. Then we go naked out-of-doors. The period of chattering teeth is past. No matter what the weather is we go calmly out into it, lie down in the drift, look up into the sky, and then scrub ourselves with snow. It's the finest bath in the world.

It rains to-day—or snows. The snow lies three feet deep on the level. At our windows it is above the sills. In Seward,—have I written this before?—it lies so deep that one can't see across the street. The snow is the deepest, and that last cold snap the coldest, of any winter remembered or recorded. The cold was very many degrees below zero. So we have experienced a true winter. We're so glad to know it.

Tuesday, February Eighteenth

Such mild weather! With the fire nearly out it's hot indoors to-night. A little snow, a little rain, but altogether a pleasant day. It's always pleasant when I paint well. To-day I redeemed two straying pictures and they're among the elect now. To-night a steamer entered from the westward, the Curacao long expected. She must have been here two or three days ago and since then been to Seldovia. With incredible slowness she crept over the water. What old hulks they do put onto this Alaskan service.

Rockwell's mothering of all things exceeded reason to-day. He put two sticks of wood on the fire after I had intended it to go out. I removed them,

SIR
LANCELOT
of the
LAKE

And in all the world there
was no other knight so
brave, so gentle or of
such renown.

165

blazing merrily. "Don't" cried Rockwell seriously, "you'll hurt the fire's feelings."

Rockwell cleared off the boat to-day. Next we must dig her out. To-morrow the engine must be put in order. We must find a hole in the gasoline tank and solder it and then coax it into starting. It is on such jobs that whole precious days are wasted.

Rockwell loves every foot of this spot of land. To-night he spoke of the beauties of the lake, its steep wooded shores, clean and pebbly, and the one low, clear, and level spot where we approached the water. He had planned to live this summer the day long on the shores of the lake, naked, playing in and out of the water or paddling some craft about. I thought of putting up a tent in some mossy dell along the shore and letting Rockwell sleep there nights alone and learn early the wonders of a hermit's life. And none of it is to be!

WEDNESDAY, FEBRUARY NINETEENTH

It rains and storms. But to-day we repaired the engine and we're ready to start for Seward when it clears. Above every other thought now is the sad realization that our days on this beloved island are nearing an end. What is it that endears it so to a man near forty and a little boy of nine? We have such widely different outlooks upon life. It may be that Alaska stands midway between us, and that I, turning backward from the crowded world that I have known and learned to fear, meet Rockwell in his forward march from nothing—to this. If that be so we have met only for a moment for such perfect sympathy. His love will pass on from this and mine will grow dissatisfied and wander still. But I think it's otherwise. It seems that we have both together by chance turned out of the beaten, crowded way and come to stand face to face with that infinite and unfathomable thing which is the wilderness; and here we have found OURSELVES— for the wilderness is nothing else. It is a kind of living mirror that gives back as its own all and only all that the imagination of a man brings to it. It is that which we believe it to be. So here we have stood, we two, and if we have not shuddered at the emptiness of the abyss and fled from its loneliness, it is because of the wealth of our own souls that filled the void with imagery, warmed it, and gave it speech and understanding. This vast, wild land we have made a child's world and a man's.

I know nothing in all life more beautiful than the perfect belief of Rockwell in his Paradise here. Unopposed, his romance has kindled every object

166

on the homestead; so that now for hours he can steal about in the forest, on the beach, along the lake,—in absolute contentment, for it is wonderland itself. The "King's road," the "Giant's path" where stand the gummy "ten-pound butter tree" and all the giants with whom Sir Lancelot must joust, the magpie's grave marked with a cross, the otter's cave, the marvelous frozen stream; those strange wild people, the Treaps, who visit these shores occasionally to hunt the white man for his skin as the white man has hunted their dear animals; rain-bears and wild-cat-eaters—appalling animals that inhabit the dark woods but are good friends to Rockwell. Every log and rotten stump, the gnarled trees, with or without "butter," every mound and path, the rocks, the streams, each is a being in itself; and with those most living goats, and the brilliant magpies, the pretty, little dingy sparrows, the glorious and virtuous porcupines, the black, black crows, the great and noble eagle, the rare spider and the rarer fly, and the wonderful, strong, sleek otters that leap in sport through the snow and coast down-hill, they make a world of romance that has thrilled one little boy to the very bottom of his soul. To live here, to accumulate about him more and more animals and shelter them from harm, to live forever or, if he must, grow old, and very old; here marry—not a Seward girl but one more beautiful—or an Indian!—here raise a great family—and here die. That now is the ideal of little Rockwell. And if we, his family, all of us, would count we must come here to him where with patriarchal magnificence and dignity he will care for us.

Thursday, February Twentieth

All day out-of-doors, both of us. In the morning Rockwell and I journeyed around the point between the two coves of the island. It's a rocky promontory with a great jumble of bowlders at its base that one must scramble over. These are generally wet and slippery and not much fun. However we went well around and I set up my canvas and painted while Rockwell crawled about in caves and crevasses playing some sort of wild beast. The wind rose as I finished and made it difficult to convey my wet canvas without damaging it. And in the afternoon again I painted on two pictures out-of-doors. That's to be my work now till the time I go. To-morrow if the day is right we start for Seward. Our boat is dug out of the snow, our goods are packed, the engine chafes at the throttle. I am tired to-night and it is bedtime.

Friday was calm. We left the island at about eleven—after the usual hours fussing with the engine. At Hogg's camp we called in for something to bail with, for the boat, being leaky, had taken in a lot of water. No one at home—so I stole a bowl from the shed and we proceeded. By then the sun shone upon us and we could observe, what we later confirmed at Seward, that the sun shines at the head of the bay while the island, our island, is shrouded in clouds. Quite different conditions prevail in the two localities. With us it is warmer and much wetter. The recorded rainfall for Seward, that some time ago seemed incredibly small, does not fit Fox Island at all. Olson's records for last summer show prevailing rainy weather—and Seward rejoiced in unprecedented sunshine! And during these three days in Seward now, days wonderfully fair, thick clouds have always been over Fox Island. And even the wind blows there when Seward's waters are calm.

And so on Friday we reached Seward with flying colors stowed our boat up high, put the engine into Olson's cabin, and walked again the streets of civilization. Here everyone is friendly. The first night Rockwell dined out at one house and slept at another with a lot of children. What must they have thought of his underclothes! I went supperless—writing letters instead. And then flute music at the postmaster's. Next day very early the steamer came and the day passed for me in the wild excitement of receiving mail. *Here everyone is friendly. Next day very early the steamer came and the day passed for me in the wild excitement of receiving mail. All day it lasted. Then at five Rockwell and I go to dine with Dr. Sloane, a Scotchman, a graduate of Glascow and Edinburgh an ex professor of surgery, an Alaskan "sourdough" or old timer of varied and thrilling experience. A fine fellow full of life and good spirit. He told me of his adventures as a practitioner at Nome with a radius of one or two hundred miles to cover. Stefansson had aroused the Dr's ire at Nome. His blond-haired blue-eyed esquimaux were a joke to the Alaskans of the north. And when Stefansson returned north to seek again the blond and blue-eyed ones it was said the only such were his stray progeny. Rockwell went with two other children to the movies as Brownell's guest. Again to-day Rockwell lunched out and we dined at the Roots. Everywhere people are friendly limitless privileges and farms are offered me. I'm to have a cabin at Kenai lake—and as far as I can make out almost anything else I want. On my next visit the Chamber of Commerce wants me as their guest.*

168

him where with patriarchal magnificence
and dignity he will care for us.

Frozen Fall
N.W of Olsens cabin.

169

Isn't it ridiculous. But what a contrast to Newfoundland—or New York or any other spot I've ever landed on. And I so often observe people restraining their curiosity about me. Those who know me well have asked to see my work if I bring it here—but always without intrusion. Brownell has offered me a furnished house to live and work in free, or his own house to work or write in. Of that I have the key. The house I lived in on my last visit is still at my disposal. The town is livelier than it has been on my other visits. There are returning soldiers and men from the interior coming and going. They're a finely set up lot. The soldiers, the uniforms, and the best of what they suggest look cheap beside the big fellows of this country. It's true perhaps that the miserable city slave is set upon his feet by the discipline and experience of army life. But the strong man too often returns, always maybe, much poorer for such dirty work. I can't believe that the hardships to which the low average of men so easily adapt themselves to are any trial to a good man's strength. If the army can be justified by what it does for young men why not draft the common man and make of him during his service a woodsman, a railroad builder, a pioneer, a farmer or rancher!

Wednesday, February Twenty-sixth

Yesterday we came home! We left Seward with only a light load aboard. It blew briskly in the bay from the north. Before we reached Caine's head there was a splendid, white-crested chop racing along with us. Midway across it was about all the engine could have stood. The propeller is not set at enough depth in our boat and in yesterday's sea it was most of the time out of water, racing at a furious pace. Then the boat would naturally lose steerage way and we'd swing far out of our course. But it was great sport. Into it we could have made no headway; before it nothing could stop us. And the engine kept right on going!—only as usual it was continually falling apart. On Friday the flywheel came loose six times, the muffler four, and the valve spring fell off and stayed off. Coming back all went well till we were in the roughest sea; then the muffler came loose. Not wanting to stop the engine in that sea I spent half the time on my knees holding the tiller in one hand and the muffler nut with a pair of pliers in the other. Rockwell bailed most of the time. The boat leaks like a sieve.

And how fine to get home again! Only an hour and we were again seated at dinner in our warm cabin. Rockwell said it was hard for him to remember whether Mr. Olson or we had just been to Seward. I brought Olson a battery box and batteries as a present. He was much pleased. But particularly his mail pleased him. I saw him soon after our arrival seated with his spectacles on studying his letters. He rarely gets any. This time came a post-card and letter from Rockwell's mother.

The day passed and evening came. Then appeared entering our cove a cabined gasoline boat. Two young fellows came ashore and we all chatted in Olson's cabin. One had his wife aboard. They claimed to be hunting a stray boat,—but Olson whispered to me later, dramatically, that they were doubtless out dragging somewhere for a cache of whiskey. Lots of whiskey has been sunk in the bay. Marks were taken at the time to determine its location and now the owners as need arises fish up what they want. It's just like the buried treasure of the days of piracy. Doubtless there are now many charts extant with the position of liquid treasure marked upon them.

To-day has been again overcast but beautifully mild. It is really a wonderful climate. Rockwell makes the most of these last days. He went this morning to the ridge's top east of us, and this afternoon high up on the mountain side. He now wants to stay here and become a wild man. There is no question in my mind about his entire willingness, his desire, to be left here when I go.

XI. TWILIGHT

The first of March! If only the dull weather would clear up I could get more done these last days here. Fifteen brand-new canvases hang from my ridge pole waiting for pictures to adorn them. To-day is the only day that work out-of-doors has been quite out of the question. It snows hard. Last Thursday morning Rockwell and I began to take our morning baths in the bay—the snow having become too hard. And now at just seven-fifteen—on cloudy mornings, clothed in sneakers we scamper down the shore and plunge into the waves. Brrrrrrrr! It's cold, but mighty good. Olson, after predicting for some time a dire end to our morning performances, has at last evinced enough curiosity to drag himself out of bed and come over to see. But he has not yet been early enough to catch us.

The days are lengthening rapidly. It is now after six o'clock in the evening and our lamp's not lighted!

Last time in Seward Olson bought a lot of odds and ends of molding for picture frames. And now, with my help, all the little things that we have given him are gorgeously framed. On the little picture of himself that I painted he has what he calls a "camoflag" frame; it's made of different moldings on the four sides. Well, Olson is mighty proud of his pictures. He's really very fond of us. People in Seward say he talks of us continually. And there it is thought quite remarkable how I have managed with the "crazy" old man. I guess the craziness explains it. I picture with horror having as a constant companion here one of the fine, stalwart, shrewd, honest, wholesome-to-sterility Americans that our country likes to be so proud of.

I told Olson of Kathleen's amusement over the brusque ending of his letter, "Answer this if you feel like it—and if you don't it's all the same to me."

"Well," he said, "that's the way it is here in Alaska; if anyone don't like the way a man does he can go to Hell!"

I've heard an amusing story about Olson and his goats at a little Seward exposition at which they were shown. They put his two goats into narrow packing boxes that their dirt might not fall onto the floor of the building. Olson arrived and seeing the plight of his pets flew into a rage. He lifted them out, hurled the packing boxes out of the door into the street, and denounced the fair-committee for their abuse of animals. *"But they dirty the floor,"* said a lady. *"Those goats are just as good as you are"* was his answer. And although the whole place tumbled about the old man's ears, he won, and saw his goats given an honorable amount of freedom in a special enclosure—curtained off, "admission to see the goats ten cents,"— which notice Olson promptly disregarded, letting everyone in—and a big crowd at that—free. *"Humans,"* says the sage Olson, *"are just one kind of animal, but they're the meanest kind. Animals will fight and kill each other but they never do it without a reason."* I've already told somewhere of a famous retort of Olson's that routed a fresh Jew. This last trip in Seward the six weeks saw the end of much of his good nature. And people took advantage of the old man and teased him a lot. He'd spend his days sitting behind the stove in Hawkins' store and it was a rare chance for the clerks to torment him. One fat, rather "stylish" looking, pompous grocery clerk has always aroused Olson's ire. On this day the fun started by someone's saying. "Olson, I saw you down the railroad track last night with a strange lady. Didn't know you were a lady's man!" Chorus, "Oh, Olson, that's the kind of business you're up to here in Seward. Tell us who she was." "Yes," here put in the fat dandy, "won't you tell us, Olson, who she was?" "I will," said Olson. "Well, who was she?" "Your Wife"!

Monday, March Third

Inauguration day passed here without event. In this ideal community of Fox Island we're so little concerned with law—the only law that bears on us at all we delight in breaking—that one wonders how far no government can be carried. One goes back to first principles in such speculation, endows man again with inalienable rights or at least inalienable desires, and then has simply to wonder how much of the love of order there is in the natural man. The fact that a large proportion of mankind can live and die without any definite knowledge of the laws of the community and without ever running counter to the forces of law is sign enough that most of the law code is but a writing down of what the average man naturally wants to do or keep from doing. There's a sharp difference between such "common" law and the exceptional law that strikes at the personal liberty of a man, laws concerning morals, temperance, or that conscript unwilling men for war. In all law there is tyranny, in these laws tyranny shows its hand. The man who wants true freedom must escape from the whole thing. If only such souls could gravitate to a common center and build the new community with inherent law and order as its sole guide!—well, we have returned to the problem. A state that was truly interested in progress would dedicate a portion of its territory to such experiment. But no state is interested in anything but the gain of one class, which means the oppression of the rest. How farcical sound these days "Life, Liberty, and the pursuit of Happiness." "No government without the consent of the governed," and other old-fashioned principles. But they have still to be reckoned with till the last Bolshevik has been converted into a prosperous tradesman and the last idealist is dead. And now for Fox Island.

The weather is dull and gray—only last evening an hour before sundown the clouds suddenly vanished out of the heavens and the sun shone as warm and beautiful as on the fairest summer day. Then I sat out-of-doors and painted while the snow and ice melted and dripped all about. The mornings are cold, doubly cold it seems when in the half-light of dawn and perhaps a driving snow squall we run naked down the long stretch of beach and plunge into the bay. I work ceaselessly. Time flies like mad and the day of our departure is close.

Tuesday, March Fourth

A day of snow and rain spent by us indoors, Rockwell hard at work upon his chart of "Trobbeabl Island"—a wonderful imaginary land where his own strange species of wild animals live—and I washing and mending. My seaman's bag, damaged on its way here in the hold of the steamer, is now quite professionally patched, and the knee of my blue overalls shines with a square patch of white canvas.

Olson was welcome and spent much of the day with us. He has reread Kathleen's letter to him and is charmed with it. He feels authorized by

The Imperishable

it to keep me here longer and surely does his best to persuade me. He treasures the picture little Kathleen sent him. All these things, the letters and little trifles that we have given him will be stored away in his too empty box of treasures among a very few old letters and a photograph or two of pioneer ladies and gentlemen in the dress-up costumes of thirty years ago. These scant treasures, what a memorial of a very lonely life! He showed me to-day a photograph of Tom Crane, an old associate of his in Idaho, and two large, splendid looking women, Crane's wife and his wife's sister. The wife was frozen to death in the snow while on a short journey with her husband. He lost both feet. Olson led the rescue party bringing in with great difficulty the dead woman and then tending Crane through long, painful days until his crippled recovery.

Thursday, March Sixth

It's mighty hard work, this painting under pressure. I'm too tired to attempt more than the briefest record on this page of two days' doings. Yesterday it was gray. At sundown it cleared giving us the most splendid and beautiful sunset, the sun sinking behind the purple, snowy mountains and throwing its rays upward into a seething red-hot mass of clouds. I painted most of the afternoon out-of-doors.

To-day we bathed at sunrise, brisk and cold and clear. The morning tide was so exceedingly low that I ran dry shod clear around the north side of the cove until the whole upper bay was visible. Olson had not known it could be done. Returning we put Olson's boat into the water and Rockwell and I embarked with my painting outfit. I landed on the point I had just visited afoot. Rockwell in jumping ashore with the painter timed it badly, slipped, and fell full length into the surf of the ground swell, the dory almost riding over him. I roared with laughter—to his great fury. He rowed about in the harbor for almost two hours returning to bring me home. In the afternoon we repeated our excursion—all but the water sports—going this time to the south side of the cove. Rockwell's a good little oarsman and above all to be trusted to do as he's told to—a vice in grown-ups, a virtue in children.

Friday, March Seventh

That to-day began in snow and cloud matters not,—it ended in a glory. Olson, Rockwell, and I sat that late afternoon far out on the bay basking in the warmth of a summer sun, rocked gently on a blue summer sea. For

and the open sea. What a thrill to look again upon that far horizon! From our feet the cliff descended in a steep V shaped divide sheer down to the green ocean; and the waves curled and eddied at its base. The mountains across from us gleamed snow white against dark clouds; and what peaks!

We hurried back to Olsen who waited in the boat. That side — the crater and the more familiar mountains to the westward — hung half shrouded in fast dissolving mist. The descent was was real short. We just sat down

hours we had explored the island's western shore, skirting its tumbled reefs, riding through perilous straits right up to where the eddying water seethed at some jagged chasm's mouth. That's fine adventuring! flirting with danger, safe enough but close—so close to death. We landed on the beach of Sunny Cove, found in the dark thicket the moldering ruins of an old feed house of the foxes, gruesome with the staring bones of devoured carcasses. And then we younger ones dashed up the sheer, snow-covered eastward ridge—dashed on all fours digging our feet into the snow, clinging with hands as to a ladder. There at the top two or three hundred feet above the bay we overlooked the farthest seaward mountains of Cape Resurrection, then Barwell Island and the open sea.

Ah, to see again that far horizon! Wander where you will over all the world, from every valley seeing forever new hills calling you to climb them, from every mountain top farther peaks enticing you. Always the distant land looks fairest, till you are made at last a restless wanderer never reaching home—never—until you stand one day on the last peak on the border of the interminable sea, stopped by the finality of that.

From our feet the cliff dropped in a V-shaped divide straight down to the green ocean; and at its base the ground swell curled, broke white and eddied. The jagged mountains across shone white against black clouds,— what peaks! huge and sharp like the teeth of the Fenris-Wolf.

We hurried back to Olson who waited in the boat. That side—the cove and the more familiar mountains to the westward—lay half shrouded in fast dissolving mist. The descent was real sport. We just sat down and slid clear to the bottom, going at toboggan pace. Poor Olson, who watched us from below, was aghast. On the shore I found a long, thick bamboo pole, doubtless carried directly here from the orient by the Japanese current. We longed to go across to Bear Glacier that we could now see, a broad, inclined plane, spotless white, with the tallest mountains rising steeply from its borders. But it was too late and we returned home. The wonders of this country, of this one bay in fact, it would take years to know!

MONDAY, MARCH TENTH

On the eighth it snowed hard all day and both of us worked at our trade indoors. The ninth dawned fresh and clear and cold. It was too windy to go out onto the bay as we had intended, so, not to be entirely cheated

and slid clear to the bottom, going at a furious pace. Poor Olson, who watched us from below, was aghast. On the shore I found a long, thick bamboo pole, doubtless carried directly here from the orient by the Japanese current. I longed to go across to Bear glacier that we could now see, a broad, inclined plane, spotless white, with the tallest mountains rising steeply from its borders.

But it was too late and we returned home. The wonders of this country, of this one bay in fact, it would take years to know!

out of an excursion, we packed a bag of various supplies and set off for the ridge to the eastward.

It was glorious in the woods. New fallen snow lay upon the tree branches; the sun touched only the tallest tops, the wind rustled them now and then and made it snow again below. We came out upon the summit of the ridge more to the north than we had ever been before and from there beheld again the open sea. Nothing can be more wonderful than to emerge from the dense forest onto such a view! Right on the ridge we built a fire beneath the arched roots of a large tree. Rockwell will long remember that wonderful chimney beneath the roots. I painted on one of the canvases I had brought while Rockwell played about or cut wood for the fire. Presently the can of beans that we'd laid in the ashes went pop!—and we knew that dinner was ready. So we sat down and ate the good beans, bread and peanut butter, and chocolate,—while our backs sizzled and our bellies froze. But we loved it and Rockwell proposed that we spend three or four days there like that. Then after more painting and some play in the snow we came home again.

But the beautiful days must be busy ones for me. I painted out on the lake for an hour or more; after that again—this time the glorious sunset. After supper bread to bake and then, tired out, early to sleep in our great, hard, comfortable bed. Olson would have started to-day had the weather been moderate. But it has blown fiercely from the north—and still it blows. All day I worked packing and now my boxes are made and nearly filled. It is surely true that we are going! All day it has seemed to me to be fall. We had thought of that before during these recent days. We scent it and feel it. I believe that it's the end of a real summer in our lives that we taste the sadness of.

TUESDAY, MARCH ELEVENTH

It blows incessantly, cold and clear,—blue days. I have painted most of to-day, first indoors, and then outdoors commencing a large picture. Olson has been with us much of the time. He treasures every little memento we can give him. In his pocket-book are snapshots of Kathleen, Clara, and Barbara. He wanted Barbara's curl that I have—but I couldn't give him that. It looks as if we should all go to Seward together. This wind is likely to hold until the full moon passes—and that's still some days off. My trunk is about packed and what remains can be done in a very few hours.

Speaking to Olson to-night about the possibility of a shipwrecked man

built a fire beneath the arched roots
of a large tree. Rockwell will
long remember the wonderful chimney beneath

the roots. I painted on one of
the canvases I had brought along
while Rockwell played about or cut
wood for the fire. Presently the
can of beans that we'd laid in
the ashes went pop! — and we
knew that dinner was ready. So we
sat down and ate the fine dinner
of beans, bread and peanut butter and

being able to support life on this coast for any length of time he told of a native boy of Unga, "crazy Simyon," who lived four years at Nigger Head, a wild part of Unga Island, with no shelter but a hole in a sand bank, no fire, no weapons or clothes, or tools; a first-hand story, long, wild, terrible, beginning with a boy's theft of sacrificial wine, and ending in madness and murder. "Simyon" as a boy was left an orphan. He was wayward and ran wild in the settlement. At last he broke into the Russian church there and got drunk on the sacramental wine. He was detected and, while not actually punished, so frightened by the threat of hanging for his enormous crime that he fled, and finally reached Nigger Head. After his disappearance four years passed. One day a fisherman going to Nigger Head from his camp nearby saw the print of naked feet in the sand. Next day he returned armed and, following the tracks, discovered the burrow in the sand. At the point of the gun Simyon was forced to show himself. He was a wild figure now of man's stature. Long, unkempt hair hung about his shoulders and he was naked but for a loin cloth. He spoke good English and told his story from the beginning. Through those four years he had lived upon sea-eggs picked up on the shore and slept in a bed of dry grass. The fisherman took Simyon with him to the nearest camp. Here lived a man named Tibbits and his wife. As they neared the camp the fisherman called out "Tell your wife to hide herself—and bring me some old clothes." Well, they dressed up Simyon, washed him—we hope—cut his hair, and kept him with them till the season's end. He was a good hard worker. Then all of them returned to Unga. Simyon, not well received here by his own race. He drifted finally to Sand Point and got into company with another native named Simyon. Across a stretch of water from Sand Point lived a Scandinavian and his native wife. This man, P - - - - -, was of middle age and a worthless drunkard. His wife, still young, had been married to him while quite a girl and against her will. He kept her with him by force. Her own reputation was however far from good. The two Simyons crossed over the water to where P - - - - - and his wife lived. They carried plenty of drink along. They disposed of P - - - - - and left the rest to their own devices. That night or the next as it came to bed time all four sat in the cabin. There were two bunks. The two Simyons crawled into one of them as if to retire. P - - - - - sat at the table still drinking. And as he sat there the young men in the bunk carefully aimed their gun at him and shot him through the heart. The next day they carried out the body and laid it on a board. "Crazy Simyon" crossed to Sandy Point and going to the store

The Star-Lighter

asked for some white cotton cloth. "What do you want it for?" asked the storekeeper. "To cover up the body of P - - - - -" was the ingenuous reply. At the time "Crazy Simyon" told that the other men had fired the gun. The wife was there as witness and escaped prosecution for lack of evidence against her. The Simyons received ten and fifteen years, "Crazy Simyon" dying before the expiration of his term. P - - - - -'s wife, Annie, returned to Unga from Valdez when the trial was held bedecked with finery and with a heavy purse—the wages for her detention at the trial. She married a young Norwegian fisherman, trapped with him for a while, but died within a few years. Olson knew all the characters of this story well, was at Sand Point at the time of the murder and refused the job of guarding the prisoners.

WEDNESDAY, MARCH 12TH, FOX ISLAND

Olsen hurried in out of the blustering wind and cold. "Here's a story," he said, "about two young fellows—that will show you the kind of sailors we have here in Alaska. When they struck gold on the beach at Nome of course everybody all over the country got excited. Down at Unga the miners and everybody else wanted to quit and get right up to Nome. There were two young fellows had a small schooner over at Sand Point and they wanted in the worst way to get up North. At last they got together an outfit consisting of a sack of flour, a ham, two cases of beer, a cat with six kittens and a cod fish line, loaded it aboard the schooner and set sail for Unga. It was blowing pretty stiff and when they got to Kelly's Rock they'd sailed a mast right out of her. However, they rigged up enough sail on the other one to carry them on to Unga. There they put in another mast, celebrated a bit around the town, and then with everybody watching them and seeing them off they got aboard again and set sail for Nome. Sweeney was the name of the one that owned the boat. He was a Swede and his right name was Swanson. So he was captain. The other fellow was named Hospital Gus because whenever anything was being done at the hospital at Unga he was there to work. Well, he was the crew of the schooner. They had sailed only a little way and were still in clear view of the watching town when along came a "white squall." "Shorten sail!" called out the captain. "No, let her crack on" answered Hospital Gus. So the squall struck them and as the schooner had no ballast she turned right over and lay with her keel in the air and her sails all set down in the water. But the captain and the crew got up onto the keel and

MARCH 5151

Dearist Mothere
I hope you are stil
harving a grate time
We will be back prity
soon. and I will
sho you chou to write
betr. I will sho you
the chole ABC in writing nou
A b c d e f g h i j k l m n
o p q r s t u v w x y z.
Father is packing the trungk
to day.
I'm going to bring lots of
shels and fethers.

GIVE THIS MUCH LOVE TO THE
CHILDREN AND TO YOUR SELF
120,140,180 330 809. 100,100,
100,101,102,13 6,00,
LOVINGLY ROCKWELL

186

MARCH 13

DEARIST MOTHER
Yestuday it was nirly the
codist day we harve had.
And I played dominoes.
while Father painted outside
nirly all daylong.
MARCH 13TH.   I STADE
in the chouse and warked
on an olden map.
In the evrening it got
wormr. I went out to play
dominoes

MARCH 14TH
THE   CALLEST   DAY.   NOTHING TO
SAY
WE   HAD   THE BEST ICE
CREAM.   I LIKE TO HEAR MR OLSON'S
AND MR KENT'S   STORYES   THE
TELL   NICE   STORIES
              LOVINGLY   ROCKWELL

5 MARCH 2 ND

Dearest Mother :—

THE THIRD DAY IN SEWARD

T he women in the hotel gave me som ice kream

T hen we talk to gather and S he siad all of the boys were in school but I wad finde some boy to play with

S o I went out to hunt for a boy to play with.

A nd I found a boy called fransie. and we found a dog sleigh and a lot of other boy played with us

A ll of the boys were dogs ksept one was the driver

A nd I was the leader.

A ll the time the driver was saying GO LEADER — GO LEADER — GO LEADER — GO LEADER.

T hat night Father and I went to

HOGS ROOTS. THE END LOVINGLY : ROCKWELL KISIS

188

sat there till a launch from Unga towed the whole outfit back. The schooner was towed up onto a bar—and there, since they had no money to pay for her salvage, she was let to lie. Sweeney was the only one of the two that ever got to Nome, and that was two years later. And when he'd been there a little while he committed suicide."

This has been one of the winter's very cold days. Nevertheless the day was passed as usual of late with the ocean bath to begin with, out-door painting most of the day, and reading to Rockwell and writing at night. Right now it is bitterly cold and the wind blows without pause. And it is bed time.

Thursday, March Thirteenth

Last night was bitterly cold. I had to get up repeatedly to attend to the fire. The wind howled and the vapor flew and Rockwell and I hugged close together beneath the blankets. Day dawned still icy cold. By noon it began to snow and the afternoon was calm and mild. And now again the wind blows fiercely from the northeast and we're freezing cold! The day was spent in packing. The dismantled cabin looks forlorn.

Sunday, March Sixteenth

With the full moon has come the most perfect calm. If it holds through to-morrow we shall leave the island. The past three days have been busy ones. Bitterly cold weather has prevailed with the wind unceasingly from the north—almost the coldest days of the winter. Still I did some painting out-of-doors every day until yesterday, trying hard to pin upon the canvas a little more of the infinite splendors of this place. Meanwhile our packing was carried on. We have made a thoroughly good job of it—I hope! But who can tell what strain a trip of so many thousand miles will put upon our crates and bundles? But for a promise we had made Olson to go with him to Sunny Bay and Humpback Creek—on the eastern mainland— we'd have gone this day to Seward.

By noon the most perfect calm had settled upon the water. The sky was cloudless, and although really it was still very cold the bright sun looked like warmth—and that helped a lot. So Olson's little engine, sputtering, stammering, stopping a great deal, carried us upon our trip. At Humpback Creek there are falls maybe thirty feet high, perfect falls tumbling sheer down from a plateau into a deep round basin. The falls to-day were frozen and spread wide over the face of the cliff; but it was

189

I , might have lived had we not
met Olsen that fair Sunday in August.

A little cabin stood there - open to
the weather through doorway and window but
otherwise snug and comfortable. Still
even with that _great_ wonder, the fall,
so near that spot was not to
be compared with our own Ice Island
home. Next we went to Sunny
Bay to visit the old trappers who h-

easy to imagine the grace of their summer form. We had to hurry from here or be stranded by the rapidly retreating tide. Next we went to a spot on the bay where Rockwell and I might have lived had we not met Olson that fair Sunday in August. A little cabin stood there—open to the weather through doorway and window but otherwise snug and comfortable. Still, even with that great wonder, the fall, so near, that spot was not to be compared with our own Fox Island home. Next we went to Sunny Bay to visit the old trapper who has been wintering there—the same who stopped last fall at our island while on his way to camp. The old fellow came to meet us as we landed, a feeble, emaciated figure. He has been sick all winter and has done practically no trapping. What a forlorn latter end for a man! He drags himself about each day, cuts wood, lugs water, cooks, and when he stoops dizziness overcomes him. He sets a small circle of traps and drags himself around to tend them. His whole winter's work is twelve ermine and two mink—thirty or forty dollars' worth at the most. We offered to bring the old man back with us and from here on to Seward—but he preferred to stay there a few days longer.

And now I sit here with our packed household goods about me, empty walls and a dismantled home. Still we hardly realize that this beautiful adventure of ours has come to an end. The enchantment of it has been complete; it has possessed us to the very last. How long such happiness could hold, such quiet life continue to fill up the full measure of human desires only a long experience could teach. The still, deep cup of the wilderness is potent with wisdom. Only to have tasted it is to have moved a lifetime forward to a finer youth. *How long such a life could continue to charm one of course cannot know; but it is clear to us now as we leave it that we have only begun to know the wonders of the life and of the land. We are both resolved in our hearts to return here and explore freedom to its limits—truly a life time's plan. We have learned what we want and are therefore wise. As graduates in wisdom we return from the university of the wilderness.*

Tuesday, March Eighteenth

Fox Island is behind us. Last August Olson picked us up as strangers and towed us to his island; yesterday, after nearly seven months there with him we climbed again into our dories and crossed the bay—and now we extend the helping hand to the old man and tow him and his faltering engine back to Seward. The day dawned cold and windy. We proceeded

191

sea. —— And now at last it _is_ over. Fox Island will soon become in our memories like a dream or vision, a remote experience too unreal, for the free beings we knew there and the deep peace, to be remembered or believed in as a real experience in life. It was for us life as it should be, serene and wholesome, love — but no hate, faith without disillusionment, the absolute for the earth-striding footsteps of man and for his soaring spirit. — Olson of the deep experience, strong, brave, — generous and gentle like a child, — and his island — like Paradise. ——————— Ah God, — and now the world again!

192

however at once to the completion of our packing and the loading of the boat.

A little after noon the wind moderating slightly we persuaded Olson to come with us. My engine working beautifully carried both boats along till the other little motor could be prevailed upon to start. In the bay the wind was fresh and the chop high. Half-way across the wind had risen and the water flew. Olson's engine worked so poorly that most of the time I had the full strain of his dory on the line. I feared the old man's courage would give out as the sea increased, and I grinned at him reassuringly from time to time. Finally, however, as the white-crested waves seemed to rush ever more fiercely upon us his face grew solemn. He waved to us to turn and run back to the island. But the tow line was fast in my boat and I neither chose to turn nor loosen it. Showing our backs to him we ran for the shelter of Caine's Head—and made it. From there onward we skirted the cliffs and found it smooth enough. The wind again died out and we entered Seward over a glassy sea.

And now at last it is over. Fox Island will soon become in our memories like a dream or vision, a remote experience too wonderful, for the full liberty we knew there and the deep peace, to be remembered or believed in as a real experince in life. It was for us life as it should be, serene and wholesome; love—but no hate, faith without disillusionment, the absolute for the toiling hands of man and for his soaring spirit. Olson of the deep experience, strong, brave, generous and gentle like a child; and his island—like Paradise. Ah God,—and now the world again!

The Magpie's Grave.

THE MAD HERMIT

INTRODUCTION

Of a winter (that of 1918-1919) spent on a fairly remote Alaskan island in the companionship of my nine year old son, my book, *Wilderness*, is the record. It was an experience so memorably happy for us both that I need the reminder of these drawings to recall that there were hours when the elder of the two became so poignantly aware of his adult solitude as to indulge himself in picturing a hermit's life as from fragmentary experience he imagined it might be—the hermit's moods as wind, as sky and ocean depths, as mountains, stars and the impendent Universe, not Man, engendered them; in picturing the hermit's *growth* toward a comprehension of the universal heartlessness but for the heart of Man. And Man, in that stark universe, as his own self—his understanding being, somewhat as Berkeley held, its Sun.

Of such indulgence these seven drawings were the fruit—in proper irony to be entitled, when they were subsequently shown, *The Mad Hermit* series.

—ROCKWELL KENT

The Hermit

Ecstasy

Pelagic Reverie

Prison Bars

Running Water

Immanence

The Vision